SURVIVAL ON A CORAL PLANET

BILLIE R. ARMSTRONG
CASU-F 20 IN WW II - 1943 - 1946
US NAVY

Planet definition; Isolated, Remote, Island! Land surrounded by water

Part 1- Into the Breach

My first journey toward reality began in San Diego, California the 9th of October 1942 when I enlisted into the United States Navy, a real jolt into the world of reality was in store for this naïve young dreamer, who had no concept of the horrors of war that awaited him in the month's to come.

Being a southern California boy, I was not ready for the cold reality of winter. My closest contact with snow was the Laguna Mountains, 60 miles east of my home in San Diego, so it was quite an introduction to the cold and brisk winter of Idaho, and the next few weeks would become quite an adventure for this young fellow.

A few weeks later, into the latter weeks of November, as I slept in our second story barracks, Mother Nature descended with a fury. During the night the snow had begun and the upstairs windows were completely covered. Nothing was visible outside, as the drift had completely covered that side of the barracks with the heaviest snow in this area in over 50 years, ah! What joys' awaited us? How I wished for the warmth of my home in California.

Boot Camp-Farragut, Idaho 1942

Finishing up in mid-December, I was given 2 weeks leave, after which I was transferred to Bremerton, WA then to Kirkland, WA, waiting for the completion of the USS Chincoteague AVP-24 (a small seaplane tender), which was commissioned in April 1943.

Photo # 19-N-57482   USS Chincoteague on 27 December 1943, port bow view

"U.S.S. Chincoteague, shown off of Mare Island after completing repairs due to Bomb damage incurred at Vanikoro, Island in July 1943"

"Crossing the Equator June 1943, King Neptune, and his Crew!
U.S.S. Chincoteagourtue-AVP-24"

Making of a Sailor" June 1943 crossing the Equator, and its results, initiation
the ordeal,
Making of a Shell Back"

After a short shakedown cruise we set sail from San Diego, California on Sunday the 13th of June for a destination that was a mystery to all except our skipper.

We arrived in the Hawaiian Islands Oahu Sunday the 20th of June and after we had received a large contingent of Sailors and Marines aboard, we departed on the afternoon of June 22; we headed out again, destination and address unknown!

After crossing the equator, we Pollywogs went through our initiation to become Shell Backs, (Full fledge Sailors), and then we reached Wallace Island's on the afternoon of June 30 1943.

After discharging a large number of Sailors, Approximately 50 or so, we again headed out on July 1st with the remaining group of Marines still aboard. The Chincoteague, AVP 24 arrived July the 4th 1943 in Espiritu Santos, and shortly after arriving at our anchorage, the remainder of our passengers, the Marine unit, were dispatched to their destination.

Our skipper, Commander Ira E. Hobbs reported aboard the Mackinac, AVP 13 to confer with that ships Commanding officer, Commander Paul D. Sropp, this meeting was observed by Lt. (jg) John K. Myhre in the bridge area of the Mackinac. During this period, Commander Hobbs conferred with the skipper of the Thornton, AVD 11. Lt. Frank D Langworthy SOM2/c and James W Beall witnessed this conference in the bridge area.

During that period of time, when Commander Hobbs was aboard the Thornton, James Beall would be a witness to the conversation between there Skipper, Commander Sellers and Commander Hobbs of the Chincoteague. During this conversation, Sellers was explaining his choices for an anchorage at the Island of Vanikoro.

He believed the choice Hobbs was about to make was a mistake as to where his anchorage would be, or the prudent one, due to those experiences that he had encountered as Captain of the Thornton.

He stated that the restrictive space that he would encounter in the smaller confines of Saboe Bay would in his opinion not serve him well in a crisis situation and would place his ship, and crew in an unpleasant situation during an attack by Japanese forces, either by air or sea. During their tour of duty in those waters they encountered the presence of Japanese Submarines with sonar soundings when they left the harbor, for whatever reason, they would send a PBY aloft to scout the surrounding area adjacent to there position, and would be at flank speed while leaving the confines of the larger anchorage. On numerous occasions submarines had been sighted from aircraft going and returning to the anchorage. With no surveillance outside the anchorage of Saboe Bay, their situation would become tenuous at best. During the evening hours nothing would be in place to intercept, or prevent a submerged Submarine from entering the harbor and inflicting a mortal blow to any ship that was anchored within the smaller confines, as there was not enough room to maneuver the ship at that darkened time. Even if they became mobile, an exit from that area would be almost impossible to navigate out through the narrow channel during those hours would be suspect at best!

Returning back to those days more than sixty three years ago when, as a seventeen year old raw recruit that placed his fortunes within the hands of older, and wiser men, it is very difficult to rationalize in my mind the decisions that were made then would have such disastrous result on so many lives, including my own.

The documentation that has been collected and included within the pages of this book were somewhat of a shocking nature, and changed my prospective of those persons that I had trusted to make the right choices while performing their duties, and what impact those decisions would have on the families of those that did not return from the war! I must admit that this discovery has had a deep and sorrowful impact on me, but there is no way we can change history, only the way in which we view those persons that were involved in it!

Commander Hobbs had received just about the same cautions from Commander Sellers of the Mackinac, and he made his own choice!

We departed the following morning at approximately 11 AM for Vanikoro Island, in a relief capacity, replacing the Mackinac as a servicing vessel for the PBY Patrol Squadron stationed there.

It should be remembered that the Mackinac, in conjunction with the Thornton, had decided to use the larger anchorage at Peou Bay for their aircraft servicing duties, because there was a larger area for maneuvering the ship in case of attack by Japanese forces. It also offered a larger extended range for radar surveillance and the ability to execute a hasty retreat from danger.

The Commanding Officer of the Mackinac tried to explain how vulnerable they would become at that location and why they believed the larger expansive area offered a more secure choice, due to the ship being in closer proximity to the higher mountainous shoreline and would restrict the use of their radar unit from signals in that area. They could only receive signals from that area in the larger area directly toward the open expanses of ocean to the southeast.

The Thornton and Mackinac, along with the U.S.S Ballard AVD 10 would be exchanging Air-Craft Tending on a rotational basis on average every three to five weeks and had decided to use the larger outer harbor for its plane servicing duties. And for what reasons we will probably never know, as the more secluded anchorage of Saboe Bay was smaller in area, and could only be reached by traversing a narrow opening inside the reef and also was closer to the Island's shore with less room for navigation so the more sheltered anchorage was chosen by Commander Hobbs.

The Mackinac had for some time been at Espiritu Santos, forming up with a convoy to return to the United States west coast for overhaul. The ship departed from Espuritu Santos on the 9th of July 1943 and arrived there on the 25th of that month.

" Crew of the Thornton on Vanikoro Island, sometime in 1944"

"*U.S.S.Thornton, at Vanikoro Island, Santo Cruz Group*"

"*Innocence Lost, the terror that is War!*

Each person's life is a special journey, their own road to travel unique, only to them like their fingerprint no two are alike.
Remembering back to that time I recall at age seventeen this excitement to journey off into the great adventure of WW ll.
In my mind this was not a violent conflict, but a great crusade, adventure, excitement, and in this adolescent teenage mind, what an awakening and surprises, realties, lay ahead for this less than mature young boy, for in just a few short months that childish look at what I had perceived to be a wondrous, exciting journey, and adventure, became a frightening nightmare of violence, and death, so this was to become the start of my own journey on this road of life!
Billie R. Armstrong.

We arrived on July 6, 1943. The work proceeded without incident, until the afternoon of July 14th. On that day at about 12:30 pm a plane, believed to be on a photographic mission, was sighted at an altitude of approximately fifteen thousand feet.

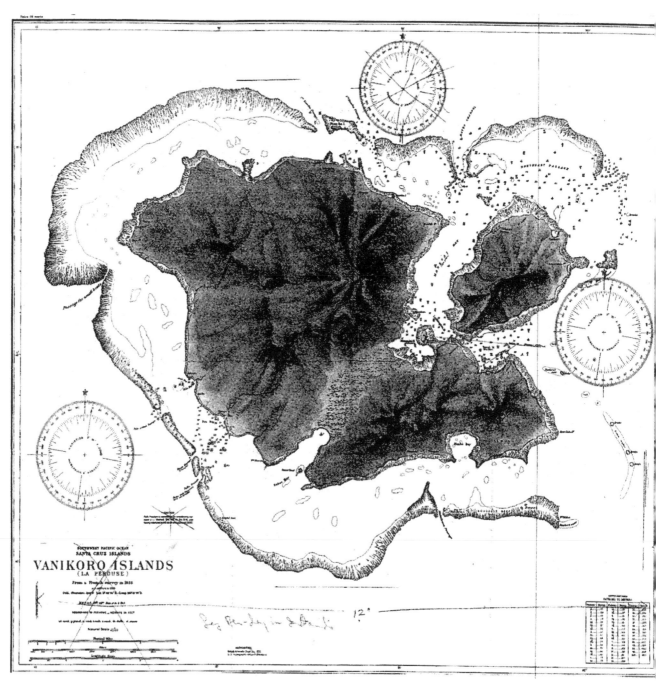

"A Map of the Vanikoro Islands"

Fire was opened up almost immediately, but the results were undetermined. The ship had left its' anchorage in the harbor and proceeded to the safety of the open sea and remained there for about one hour before returning to the anchorage after losing contact with the plane.

Normal routine was continued through the rest of the day and during the next until 06:47 pm in the evening when a Japanese twin-engine bomber was picked up on radar. The plane, believed to be a Sally type, after circling about for some few minutes, dropped two brilliant white flares about two thousand yards off port quarter from an altitude of approximately fifteen hundred feet. These flares landed near the entrance of Saboe Bay. During this time no gunfire was used in order to take full advantage of the darkness and to keep our position hidden. Contact was lost shortly after the flares were dropped, and life aboard the ship returned too normal.

On the morning of the sixteenth at 07:17, five Japanese twin engine bombers were picked up on radar circling the bay and then sighted overhead. They released their bomb loads from an altitude of about eight thousand feet. The bombs fell about fifteen hundred yards from the ship, bursting in the jungle to the east of Saboe Bay entrance. Only this one run was made, the planes continued on out of contact.

A few hours later at 11:10, another formation was picked up on radar. This group made a dummy run on the ship and these were thought to be a Sally type and this time there were nine of them flying a close V formation. On this run they passed on the starboard side, heading out to sea.

After circling about, they came in from the sea, passing this time on the portside. The ship got underway immediately by slipping the starboard anchor, and at the same time opening fire, but no bombs were dropped, and the planes disappeared eastward. Five minutes later, at 11:36 they came again and this time it was the bombing run. They dropped sticks of three bombs each in a pattern, which with our maneuvering placed two sticks on our port quarter and one directly astern. No direct hits were sustained. The closest bomb falling about fifty yards from the stern, resulting in some minor splinter damage above the fantail and to the trainers sight of number four 5"/38 gun.

The ship continued on out to sea and when contact was lost, it returned at 13:00, in order to receive VP-71 which was about to land for rest and refueling, prior to a bombing mission.

During this and all subsequent actions the guns were by local control, (each gun was controlled and directed by there own crews) as the ship had no directory control system (radar control that was not dependable at this time during the early stages of the war and was not of any great value); also during the night there had been no activity by the Japanese, but even so their would be no restful sleep during that period of time.

Early the next morning the planes of VP-71 began arriving from their overnight bombing mission. Radar had picked up their IFF identification signals as they came in; the last plane had landed at 07:25 when the first stick of bombs from five twin-engine bombers bracketed the ship across the forecastle.
They came from the Northwest, at about eight thousand feet, apparently having followed our planes all the way in.

The ship got underway at 07:26 heading out of the bay; immediately thereafter the planes came in from the Southeast on their second run.
The stick of bombs fell about fifty yards astern. The planes circled off preparing to make their third bombing run.

At 07:38, just as the ship was emerging from the mouth of the bay, the bombs struck. The nearest burst about fifty feet from the ship on the starboard side of the ship at frame 105; gasoline lines were ruptured and ignited as if they were pyrotechnics in No 1 M.W.B. (numerous splinter holes were made in the ships side). Fire parties rushed to the scene the gasoline system was blocked off between the rupture and the system below decks, and the fires were extinguished by the use of fog nozzles. Fires also started in the living compartments C-201, C-203 and were brought under control by the fog sprinkler system.

During this time, the ship was moving at flank speed and was not able to make any evasive maneuvers, due to the narrow confines of the channel between the coral reefs. Then at 07:57 the ship was clear of the reef and again was able to take evasive action; before this time the only recourse would be the changing of speeds to throw off the aim of the aircraft that were in pursuit.

At 08:05, a new attack was developing. Four planes, coming in from the starboard quarter. On this attack all the bombs fell clear, because after we were able to reach the open sea, evasive action could be taken by using flank speed and full ruder action. When all contact was lost, it was necessary to return in order to service and dispatch those aircraft from VS-71 Santos. We returned to port at 08:53, having received orders to return to Santos, we dispatched all of the patrol squadron except those that were in need of fueling. At 10:20 we weighed anchor and stood off the entrance, leaving browser boats to fuel the remaining planes.

It was our intention to return to Saboe Bay at 15:00 to pick up the browser boats and personnel. By 11:20 the ship had cleared the reefs and was maneuvering outside the harbor entrance.

Twenty-five minutes later another attack came. Five Sally's overhead released their sticks of bombs, which bracketed the ship.
A few minutes later after circling about into the sun, they came in again and it was at this point that we received a direct hit from what we believed to be a 100

K.G.delayed action bomb, which had pierced three decks, the super, main, and second before exploding in the Aft. Engine Room. All personal assigned to that area were instantly killed by the bomb blast, including the Chief Engineering Officer, as well as a fireman in the forward mess compartment.

During the lull between attacks, we had secured from General Quarters to condition 2 (an alert with less personnel at their battle stations) I had returned to the Galley/ Bakeshop area to help prepare meals, and refreshment for those crewmembers still on station at there assigned areas. During this period there had been no alert as to further air attacks from the Japanese bomber forces.

While I was working in the bakery area and standing in front of the dumb waiter (this devise was used to move food, and bake goods to the mess hall one deck below.) The explosion had occurred in the engine room, and the explosive force was so great that it ruptured the decking below the dumb waiter shaft, sending this force up the interior of the shaft, blowing open the door which I was standing in front of, striking me in the forehead and rendering me unconscious.

I was in this state for approximately15 minutes and as a result, was left with a huge black and blue lump in the middle of my forehead, about half the size of a baseball and with one hell of a headache.

A short time after the bombing, when I had regained my senses, I was curious as to what had taken place from the bomb that had struck the ship, so decided with some sense of fear to explore that area below deck (a journey that I was to regret for the remainder of my life).

I exited the galley area on the port side of the ship where the bomb had struck, and observed an opening in the deck, but was not able to see anything below due to the lack of proper lighting. I continued along the deck area until I reached the ladder down to the crew eating area, and was astounded at what was visible in the mess hall area. The explosion from the bomb in the area directly below had forced the mess hall deck into the shape of an inverted bowl, bowed upward, and not offering safe avenue across the deck, so the only choice left was to continue toward the hatch opening at the forward entrance to the mess hall. As I came to that hatch opening, I noticed a large area covered in blood and it was there that the bomb had penetrated the deck on its deadly journey into the engine room. I didn't notice any sign of an injured person in the immediate area. After passing trough the hatch, I made my way to the starboard side of the ship toward that side of the mess hall, and as I came closer to that area I noticed a compartment ahead that had an object lying on the deck, covered with a tarp. I also noticed that this object had a human form. I was somewhat hesitant to enter that area, but proceeded anyway, after a short pause. When I came closer to the object, the realization hit home that this was indeed a body, and why I continued as I did will never be clear to me, (possible some immature curiosity on my part)

I reached down and slowly moved the tarp from one end, and was confronted by a pair of feet underneath. I then slowly pulled back the other end of that tarp. I was not prepared for what I was viewing, as the body was headless, a horrible sight. Nothing in life had prepared me for this. Due to the stress from the bombings, lack of sleep, I became sick at my stomach, not only that, but I had became a fairly close friend to Herschel E. Stroud during my short time aboard the ship.

This episode viewing the horrible mutated body of a person that had befriended me during my short period of time aboard ship would have a lasting effect on me. At only seventeen years of age it would dramatically change my attitude for some months to come; no longer a childish attitude about this great adventure I had pictured just a few months ago, but a sobering realization that this was not as I had envisioned when going off to win the war.

Seems that Herschel had stepped trough the hatch at the exact moment the bomb arrived there also; what a horrible act of fate!

Number four gun went out of commission at the same time due to water damage. The ship was now moving at slower rate of speed due to the loss of the aft engine room power and was using only the starboard propeller shaft for the ships power. Furthermore, power was also lost to the steering gear and hand steering had to be used during subsequent actions.

At 14:20 another attack developed. Three bombers came on a run at eight thousand feet and on their first approach they streamed out a series of green flares, while heading into the sun, having circled around, they started their bombing run again.

The ship opened fire with all guns; again the ship was bracketed with a series of bombs, at least one five hundred pound bomb falling along the port side stopped the forward engine room. The splinters and concussion produced by this stick of bombs resulted in considerable damage to personnel, the ship and boats, one of which caught fire. The remaining guns in working order had to be manually operated. Number three five-inch gun reported that one Japanese plane had dropped out of formation trailing smoke. This was the only observed damage recorded from our defensive actions, but a PBY patrol bomber in the vicinity later verified this.

*"**Crew members, taking a brake between attacks. USS Thornton in the distance**"*

The ship lay dead in the water until a final attack occurred at 14:50. A single plane, whose bombs fell two hundred yards abeam made it; so this marked the end of attacks, although at the time more were expected.

With the after engine flooded and with some aft compartments partly flooded, and water coming through numerous openings in the hull the ship developed a heavy list to starboard; all available men, including the gun crews, were thrown into this effort to save the ship.

Nothing could be done with the aft engine room, but bucket brigades were formed in the flooded compartments at the stern and amidships. Handy Billy pumps were also pressed into action. The bucket brigades went into action at 15:0, working without letup in an effort to keep the ship afloat. That night the struggle seemed to a hopeless struggle, unless power could be restored, to allow us to use submersible pumps, but despite all efforts the water continued to rise.
It was discovered that in the forward engine room that the water level could be controlled at a depth of a few feet; an effort was undertaken to place the engines in working order, the first to respond were the generators, both the one hundred

K.W. and two hundred K.W. started. At 23:00 the main engines were turned over. After one unsuccessful attempt the next one came to life and the ship once again was underway at 23:50. After sailing, about an hour, we were picked up by the Thornton.

THORNTON (AVD 11)

"USS Thornton, AVD-11 saved the day"

That vessel sent a boat over with additional handy Billy pumps, which were immediately pressed into service. With the Thornton as escort we sailed for close to two more hours. On two occasions, during this period, electrical fires had started and were brought under control and extinguished with CO_2 in the forward engine room.

At 02:45, fire started again in the forward engine room. The inboard engine scavenging belt was seen to be filling with oil as well as diesel, it was immediately decided to shut down the engine; however, with excess amounts of oil present on the belt there was no way to secure the engine so it continued to run.

With no way to control the speed of the engine, after a few minutes the speed of the engine began to increase and was on course to self-destruction.
It was necessary to remove all personal from the engine room, while the room was in the process of being secured, in an effort to smother the fire and at the same time foam generators were set up. The Thornton again came alongside, hoses were connected to the fire mains, and foam poured into the engine room.

The fire was fought with fog nozzles and foam until about 05:45 in the morning of the 18th when the last of the foam was used up. The fire appeared to be localized, but was still smoldering.

The forward engine room was still battened down and all intakes covered by blankets and mattresses. All hands moved topside, with the exception of the bucket brigades, which continued to function in other areas. At this time all non-essential personnel were transferred aboard the Thornton, which pulled away in order to take us in tow.

At 07:40 the towline was cast off, due to what they believed to be submarine contact. The Thornton moved off and proceeded to drop two depth charges, returning when contact was lost.

Towing resumed at 09:39 and continued until 12:17. At this time the towline was cast off, with the ship listing badly to starboard; again the bucket brigades began the tasks, but the flooding could not be stopped.

"U.S.S. Chincoteague, Dead in the water from bomb explosion in engine room! July 1943"

The stern was now settling low with less than two feet of free board remaining, as the degree of list was varying between twelve and eighteen degree.

Orders were given to lighten ship, at which time torpedoes, heavy equipment, machinery, winches, and other heavy gear were jettisoned over the starboard side. A slight improvement in our list slowly began to show the results from this effort, and with the help of additional pumps flown in by P.B.Y aircraft, along with renewed effort by the bucket brigade, enabled us to check the flooding and to eventually right the ship. During this effort at 13:04, the Thornton again came along the starboard side to furnish power for the submersible pumps, and to receive our confidential and other valuable gear. She remained alongside until morning refusing to cast off.

"Angels with Gull Wings, at 17.30-PM"

"VMF-241 The Black Sheep"

On the afternoon of July 17, 1943 the squadron was informed that they were to provide air coverage for the battle stricken seaplane tender USS Chincoteague, damaged and dead in the water, alongside the USS Thornton, and Bill Pace called a meeting to discuss the plans for the following day. Pete Folger and Henry Miller worked late that night with their maps, along with the plotting boards to plan strategy for the next day, including the employment of a path finder PV-1 Ventura. With 2 or 3 hours of sleep, they grabbed a quick shave by moonlight, and started again before 3'oclock the next morning. Millers division was scheduled for departure at 04:15, but a heavy overcast had developed in the early morning hours, delaying their departure until after seven that morning. Miller and Ledge Hazelwood took off alone following along with the Ventura on instruments until they emerged out of the overcast. Their uneventful mission had began a long day in which twenty-one other pilots, all of them veterans on their first patrol mission, except Tony Eislie, who maintained a series of over lapping patrols over the stricken vessel, and if not for a quirk of nature the day may have ended just as uneventful, at least for VMF-214, if not also for the Chincoteague!

The final flight to depart Buttons late Sunday afternoon was pace's, with Jack Petit, Dick Sigel, and McCall rounding out the flight. They arrived over the Chincoteague at 17:30, which was still dead in the water alongside the Thornton, and commenced to orbit at nine thousand feet as the daylight begin to slowly fade into late afternoon light.

Seen from above them, the darkness seemed to rise up to them, so that in a few minutes the two ships on the surface below them were slowly being enveloped by the darkness that was fast approaching with the fading daylight, and all the while the four Corsairs were still bathed in the golden light of sunset.

Likewise, any aircraft at an even higher elevation would have even more sunlight, and looking up from the lower elevation, the Marine pilots from their vantage point would find themselves at a advantage and anything above them would be easy to see, enabling Jack Petit to call out a tallyho on three aircraft approaching from the north at twelve thousand feet. Pace, believing they were Ventura's, decided to lead his flight op for a visual confirmation.

To the intruders, actually Mitsubishi GCM Nell's, it must have appeared that four Corsairs suddenly have risen from the darkness below, the twin engine Nell's dumped their bombs early, much to the delight of the crews of the Chincoteague, and the Thornton, and the surprised Japanese gunners opened fire at the marines from an extreme range-more than a thousand yards. Ignoring those Japanese gunners machine gun fire, Pace continued to climb while Dick, Segal, and McCall split away and maneuvered to catch the bombers between them. The Nell's turned to the right and dived, but they were no match for the Corsairs speed, as they plunged into the rising darkness.

The Nell on the outside of the turn fell behind, and from fifteen thousand feet, Pace selected it as his target for an overhead run. It was like ducks in a pond. He came down with a full deflection shot, with just the very tip of its tail in the outside ring of his gun sight, and triggered his guns. The incendiaries found the Nell's fuel tanks and the bomber exploded in a huge ball of fire, a spectacular sight in the fading daylight.

Jack Petit rolled in next, selecting the leader of what had once been the V of three planes, but the target proved to be more hardy. Petit raked it with a steady stream and was rewarded with a trail of smoke. He reversed his course, and came back for a firing pass from the front quarter, and reversed again for a fast turn to the left. With each successive pass he achieved more hits, though not to the extent he had hammered it the first time, and much to his frustration, the badly wounded Nell reached the safety of the clouds.

At the same time, Sigel and McCall ganged up on the last Japanese bomber, which was loosing altitude fast and was barely visible as it dived into the gloom, Sigel poured solid hits into the Nell and drew smoke, but when McCall's turn came he found that he had a problem. It was April 7 all over again! his Irish luck deserted him again in the form of his guns this time; only one was working.

The whole division had tested their guns after taking off, testing each gun individually, and his had been working. Now only one gun was operating and his pass on the Japanese plane was ineffective. He was thinking the guy in the top turret has more firepower than I have!

The other fighters came around to finish off the last Nell. Dick Sigel came in for a beam run, observing no hits but noticing that his enemy's guns remained silent. No doubt he had hit his target hard on his first run, and perhaps aided by McCall's lone gun.

Finally Bill Pace made a low side run, using the last moments of twilight. He could see that the Nell was smoking, and although he was unable to confirm any hits in the darkening light. By now it was pitch black, and none of the Marines had any night flying experience or training, making any further pursuit hazardous. Pace turned on his landing lights for a visual aid and ordered his fellow pilots to form up into a formation. The newly baptized Corsair pilots formed without incident and headed for home, leaving hundreds of jubilant witnesses on two vulnerable warships below.

When they returned to Turtle Bay, Pace and his three grinning Lieutenants gave a full account of their efforts to Pete Folger in the ready tent. The exploded aircraft was witnessed by the whole group that composed the attacking forces, simplifying the confirmation of Pace's claim.

The other two Japanese bombers were smoking, when last seen heading into cloud cover, so Petit and Sigel were given credit for a probable, and after the debriefing, they walked to the evening movie to share their tale, and satisfied that they had blunted the Japanese attack.

Ten minutes later while viewing the movie, it was halted to inform them of a radio message from the Thornton that all three of the aircraft had been seen plunging into the ocean. It would take about two weeks for an official confirmation, but Sigal and Petit had their victories and an even better ending to their story.

The brief, deadly clash over the Chincoteague and the Thornton was a fitting conclusion to the squadron's transition into Corsair's. Major Louis B. Robertshaw; Operations officer for the air group, informed them that they would be returning back to combat in two days, even though the pilots had averaged less than twenty-five hours in Corsairs.

They were desperately needed to support the New Georgia campaign, now that the ground campaign had taken longer than anticipated and in the interim, Command Air Solomon's had maintained constant bombing attacks and roving air patrols against the Japanese in the area, but strong resistance from the enemy was slowly having it's effect against VMF-214's sister squadron which was an example of severe attrition. VMF-213 had, during its combat tour over Banika weeks earlier, had began with twenty-one pilots, but it now had only eleven active pilots left.

That same evening when an air attack developed at 17:34 just as the Jenkins came in sight, three Japanese bombers started a pass at the Jenkins, but just before reaching us, jettisoned the rest of their bombs as they sought to flee. Four corsair fighter aircraft from Gregory Boyingtons, V.M.F-241 Black Sheep Squadron was in hot pursuit.

I will remember all my life, what a magnificent sight after an exhausting few days, when at times you began to wonder about your ships chances to survive and to have your spirits lifted this way, as we watched those Japanese planes, one by one go down in a fiery trail of smoke in the late afternoon light.

That night the ship lay dead in the water with the Jenkins and Trevor, which had arrived 18:20, acting as anti-submarine screen.

Pumping and bucket brigades continued without stop. At 10:21 the morning of the 19th, the Thornton was forced to cast off. Heavier seas arising resulted in a pounding together of the two ships, producing leaks in the Thornton fire room.

The flooding was now under control aboard the battered Chincoteague and forward engine room fire had died out. The tug Sonoma came alongside at 11:13 with more pumping equipment.
She also had in tow a Chincoteague motor launch, containing sixteen men. These men, left behind at Vanikoro, had fueled and dispatched the three remaining planes, and then decided to head for Espiritu Santo in the open launch. The tug had picked them up while under way to help us. The Sonoma took us in tow at 12:20, from then until we arrived in port a 08:25 the morning of the 21st, nothing of consequence took place.

"The perils of war"

It was during this bombing action that I was to receive several small shrapnel wounds, due to bomb fragments penetrating the steel side of #1 5 Inch gun turret, where I was a member of the forward gun crew on the bow of the ship when a bomb exploded along the port side (left) of our position a large piece of shrapnel from this bomb penetrated the turret wall, and was ricocheting from one side to the other as I stood almost transfixed watching this molten fiery object in it's wild journey above my head from one side to the other, and it became fragmented and reduced to smaller particles on this journey.

It was some time later, when things had slowed down, that I found I had received several pieces of this metal in my body, many small fragments in both ankles, some in my chest area another in my back, and in my left hand that is still visible even today. For several years after this incident, when I was taking a shower a small sliver would work it's way to the surface of my skin, almost hair thin in size, which would remind me of those days long ago!

Due to the severe damage that we had received during the Japanese air attacks, and repairs that had to be made, while the ship was in dry-dock. There was no way to do the repairs that needed to be done to make the ship sea worthy. We had no means of propulsion due to the bomb damage in the after engine room, also the forward engine room was in such a state that the only recourse was to make the ship as sea worthy as possible while in dry dock at Espiritu-Santo.

The decision was made to repair as much of the damage hull as was possible while here, then to hoist aboard a source for electric energy (a portable diesel generator) for lights and power to operate the ships defenses, radar, fire control and other needs, Etc. Then we were to be taken in tow by an ocean going tug.

It is worth noting that after the Chincoteague's harrowing experience at Vanikoro Island, a decision had been made some time prior to that episode to replace that area as maintenance and service base, and a forward area, some 250 miles to the northwest had been chosen, during that period.

Before the Chincoteague had arrived, supplies and equipment were being relocated to this forward area in the Solomon Islands, known as Ugi Island, so this was to be the final mission from this base at Vanikoro Island.

"The long road back"

A skeleton crew was placed aboard the Chincoteague, and the remaining crewmembers were sent aboard a cargo ship, the SS Japara, a Dutch freighter bound for U.S.

We departed Espiritu-Santo Monday morning, the 9th of August 1943, arriving in San Francisco on September 11, 1943.

After arriving back in the United States, the ship was taken into Mare Island Ship Yard and placed in dry-dock for extensive repairs that would take the better part of 6 months. Just before repairs were completed, around 15 of October 1944, I was transferred to Treasure Island Receiving Station for reassignment.

Billie and Mother in San Diego, C.A.1943

While stationed at Treasure Island, I was assigned to the bakeshop for Work and due to the fact that I had some experience on the Chincoteague as a baker striker.

"Other places, sights, and, sounds."

I was made Bkr3/c. Unfortunately; I lost that rate about 3 weeks later, after overstaying my weekend liberty (2 days), while spending time in San Diego with my mother, and also partying with some friends.

On November 30, I was sent to San Pedro, California with 5 or 6 other sailors and we boarded a tanker. From there we set sail for Hawaii. Upon arriving there, I was transferred to the receiving station at Aiea, on the island of Oahu and became a member of the general work force. Here, I did all of the work details that were needed, like loading mail and supplies.

"Heading for Roi-Namur, January 1944"

Around January 20, I was to become a part of Task Force 52 aboard an AKA-6-USS Heywood transport, bound for the Invasion of the Marshall Islands.

I was not aware of this at the time, but we could only speculate about it from the rumor mill, and scuttlebutt among the crew.

The first week of February 1944, was to be my first view of a tropical paradise, which would soon be reduced to a smoldering heap of burning rubble and decaying human bodies. The sound of large guns firing from all the combined ships in the invasion force was almost ear shattering. The rumble from the Battleships 16' guns the boom of the Cruisers, 8'and 6' guns, the sharp crack from the Destroyers 5'inch guns, along with smoke and fires created from the navy and marine air forces dive bombing and machine gunning. The island was, at times, overwhelming with its scope and magnitude, an event that was not easily forgotten in one's lifetime.

<u>"Explosion of torpedo warhead storage bunker set of by satchel charge. So massive was this explosion that large sections of concrete from the bunker were sent up to a mile into the lagoon causing injuries, and damage to some ships in the harbor"</u>

When the Island was somewhat secured, I believe the third day, those not attached to any of the units and were not part of the occupational forces, were sent ashore as a group to unload supplies and ammunition.

"One of the few Japanese, prisoners taken,-February-1944"

Water filled crater was the result of the destruction of the torpedo warhead bunker 40 feet deep, and 135-feet in circumference-February-1944!

We were also helping with the removal and burial of those Japanese killed during the battle, a nasty gut wrenching business. The sights and smell of those decaying corpses is something that never leaves you no matter how long you may live. I was informed by a crewmember of one of ships approaching the Combat area, that the smell from Roi-Namur could be detected 20 miles at sea. It was apparent to me that in war, man reverts to his most Basic instincts, which is to kill and survive. Even though he has evolved over thousands of years into our so-called modern society, there is an almost animal will to survive. It is very difficult for the average person to imagine what total destruction will look like, unless they are there to view it with there own eyes.

" Growing up quickly"

I was young and had encountered, in my previous experiences aboard ship, the difference between my earlier visions and the real savagery of a world at war. This crusade, that I had envisioned like some knight riding off to avenge the brutal attack at Pearl Harbor, but I soon awakened to the realties, and brutalities that confronted us, but learning what horrors this war had waiting for us. I began to feel uncomfortable about being in this situation. It is hard to describe just what my feelings were at that time, but one thing for sure, I wanted to be in some other location. I gazed in disbelief at the death and destruction that was everywhere; to see and hear, the horrible stench that death imprints in your mind like nothing else you will encounter in your life! I would be happy when this was behind me, as there was a sick feeling deep down inside my gut. It seems very apparent that in war you don't have many choices. I was 18 years old and had to face such horrible sights within such a short period of time. Little did I know that I had become a spectator to an event that at a later date in history would become a page written with the blood and flesh of so many American and Japanese men!

The islands that were reduced to rubble and devastation from the bombardment and bombing were on Roi-Namur (a part of the Kwajalein atoll in the Marshall Islands).

" Mitsubishi G4M "Betty" Bombers"

At this time, I need to show the importance of wresting control of these Islands from the Japanese, as on December 8th 1941a large formation of 36 Mitsubishi (Betty) bombers staged their second sneak attack against the United States base at Wake Island, from their base here on Roi-Namur. These air attacks would continue on the 9th. 26 Betty bombers and again on the 10th. 26 betty bombers, always beginning at about the same time in the morning around

11:AM and 12:PM, probably leaving their bases around dawn, or just before, from their bases in the Marshall's. Again on the 9[th,] air raid by 17 bombers at 9:AM, and on the 14[th, pre]-dawn air raids by seaplanes from Wotje at 3:30AM and again on the 15th by 4-6 Mavis flying boats. These air strikes would continue the rest of the month of December until the 23rd, when Wake Island surrendered.

In another chapter, in the evolving history of the Marshall Islands contributions to the history of WW2 would be one of those not to publicized events that only appears in the annals of the National Archives, buried in history like other events, except to those that were part of that experience and treachery by the Japanese!

"Air Attacks

"Japanese Flying boat Kawanish H8K "Emily" Flying Boat"

Early in 1940, Vice Admiral Kazume, a former UCLA student,
Proposed using six Kwanish H8K " Emily" flying boats to bomb the west coast of the United States. They would depart from the Japanese Island Base of Wotje, in the Marshall Islands (about 2,300 miles west of Pearl Harbor) and

rendezvous with submarines off the coast of California for refueling, before flying off to bomb Los Angeles.

The planes would then return to Japanese controlled territory via a second refueling. This mission was canceled, due to bad weather in the refueling area. Trials run with three H8K's attacking, Hawaiian; however they caused no significant damage and no mention was made about the incident in later reports!
" Japan! The brutal, and savage enemy. "

Kwajalein Island will forever hold its place in history for the brutal treatment of Marine 2nd Raider Battalion prisoners, captured during the action on Makin Island during 17th & 18th of August 1942.

During this action, the Japanese captured 9 members of this group, and during this period, the Marines received satisfactory care during the internment there on Makin Island at the hands of their captors, and humane treatment continued for nearly a month after their transfer to Kwajalein.

Early in October, Vice Admiral Koso Abe, Marshall Island Commander, was advised that he need not send these prisoners to Tokyo because a staff officer from a higher headquarters informed him that a recently established policy permitted the Admiral to dispose of these men on Kwajalein in any manner he saw fit, Abe then ordered the Marines beheaded. A native witnessed the executions, and based on his and other testimony, in war crimes trials after the war, Abe was convicted of atrocities and hanged on the Island of Guam.

Captain Yoshio Obara, Kwajalein Commander, who had been ordered to arrange the executions, was sentenced to 10 years imprisonment and Lieutenant Hisakichi Naiki, involved in the affair, was sentenced to 5 years in prison.

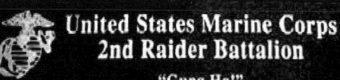

United States Marine Corps
2nd Raider Battalion

"Gung Ho!"

In memory of nine United States Marine Corps Raiders
who, by order of Japanese Vice Admiral Koso Abe,
were beheaded near this location on 16 October 1942. The
Marines were captured following their participation in the
17-18 August 1942 raid on Makin Island, and were brought to
Kwajalein and held as prisoners of war until their execution.

*It is foolish and wrong to mourn the men who died. Rather we
should thank God that such men lived.*

- George S. Patton, Jr.

"A picture of utter destruction-Namur Island-Roi Island in the background,

February 1944"

"Back to the states"

After returning to the states, in April 1944, I spent the next few weeks in limbo aboard the transport that returned me to the states, and due to the fact that I had the rank of Baker 3/c at one time, they used me in the bakery in that capacity, because they were short a rated baker at that position, but within a few days, a Second and third class Baker were transferred aboard and because I was the least senior person in that department I was transferred to Camp Elliott near San Diego and spent the next two months there working in the bakeshop.

" Return to Roi-Namur"

" Once again I return to Roi-Namur Islands, October 1944"

Once again, I was sent back to Hawaii, as a part of replacement draft. I was placed aboard the U.S.S. St. George, as one of the replacement personnel for CASU (F) 20. On this voyage I would spend my 19th birthday (no cake or candles).

An amusing incident was to occur during my return voyage back to Roi Namur Islands. One morning a couple of days out of Hawaii, I made my way back to the fantail (stern, rear) of the ship. There, I observed a sailor busy pulling a large line from the ocean that had one, or two pieces of clothing attached to the end. Now, my curiosity got the better of me so I asked him what he was up to, and at about that time one or two other persons arrived and he stated that he had tied his clothing to this piece of line and let it trail behind the ship and this was an excellent way to wash his clothes, pointing at the pieces that he had just retrieved from the line, which were sparkling clean.

The other fellows, that had just walked up, were amazed at how clean the ocean wash had made the garments and asked him to wait as they also would like to take part in this new venture. They went below to retrieve their dirty laundry. After they returned with their dirty garments and a few pieces of string to secure them to the larger line. There was quiet a bundle of goods attached to the end, so slowly they lowered the line back behind the ship at a distance of probably 75-100 yards. You could observe those items flopping around in the wake of the ship and everyone that had taken part in this enterprise, looked at each other like they had just robbed the bank and gotten off with all the money. Alas! the next morning, back on the fantail, there was a terrible commotion, and cussing going on. As I approached I was able to observe this group desperately trying to retrieve the line that was trailing behind the ship with their washing attached, but no amount of cursing, tugging, or pulling on the line helped. The ships speed was about 12 knots, and with the drag of all that clothing on the other end of the line, nothing moved. When the ship finally began to slow its speed a few days later and the line retrieved, what once had been clothing, there only remained a few scraps of non-recognizable cloth. A hard lesson learned! We landed at Kwajalein Island (about the second week of October 1944), and just about a week later we were sent across the lagoon, about 20 miles to Roi-Namur Islands, from hence the name, "THE CORAL PLANET."

I can remember approaching the island from the lagoon side. It was really a shocking sight to see a flat strip of white coral, just a few feet above the water. There was not a blade of grass or any thing green growing on this piece of war ravaged coral, with two thousand miles of ocean in each direction. As I recalled Namur Island was the island that before the invasion had trees and brush, but was void of any of these items now, due to the complete restructure that had taken place after the bombing.

"Mess hall, Chief's Mess, Galley, Bake shop, fresh water evaporator System"

*" **The gourmet sweatshop on Roi-The corrugated oven, October 1944**"*

       After going ashore we were welcomed by our new Commanding Officer, then sent to our living quarters, which were constructed from fabricated corrugate steel sheets with a curved roof and straight sides, no windows, only screened openings along the sides with a screened door at each end.

       On the outside of the Quonset hut, the openings were covered with canvas awnings that could be rolled down over the screens to keep out the rain, which when it started was sudden and torrential. Sometimes as much as 2 or 3 inches in 30 minutes, then 15 minutes later there was not a drop left on the coral sand.

       The hut was equipped with steel bunks, two people, and one over the other. Due to the location, just a few degrees above the equator with little or no shade, I never had a need for a blanket, and most of the times not even a sheet. I was assigned as a cook's striker (there was no opening bakeshop). What a piece of art this place turned out to be. There was a large double Quonset hut on one end, separated by a half wall, where the bakeshop was located, but with only _ a

Quonset hut to work in. The oven dough mixer and workbenches were on the galley side and against the south wall, from one end to the other, were the ovens with grill tops. These ovens used fuel oil as a cooking source. No windows, only a screen opening for ventilation. On the east side was the chef's mess hall, which completely closed off any air circulation to give some relief from the heat generated from the cooking fires.

Another item worth mentioning and even today I still wonder why there were not any type of fan to at least move the air around. Just a slight movement would have been a great help, as later we would learn that many of the Officers quarters were so equipped. Also, to the west side of the galley was our supply Quonset hut, where they kept food stores, canned foods, dry staples etc. Enclosed directly in front of our cooking area was the diesel generator that supplied our electricity, and this had all the airflow, in most cases blocked off, (a tribute to Military engineering and planning). Cooking inside this corrugate metal oven was really an experience in the art of sweating, especially when you were grilling on the range top. You had to have a towel around your neck, to absorb the sweat that continuously streamed down your face and into your eyes. All of your clothing would become soaking wet with your sweat.

After about 2 months, I took the examination for the rank of SC 3/c and shortly after that an opening became available for a night duty cook, whose job was to make ready the many items that were to be used in the next day's meals. This meant that I would start my days work around 7.00 pm till 12.30 or 1.00 am in the morning. This arrangement worked out very nice, as by then the temperature had dropped quite a bit and sleeping was a lot better in the Quonset.

Another one of my night cooking duties, required that I make up flight rations for the patrol and bombing flights that were going out each day, I soon found out that by making a few changes in the content of rations, a few perks came my way. The food was supposed to mainly consist of bread, sliced lunchmeat (the service men had a name for this popular food, something to do with a male horses body part), also steaks, pork chops, bacon, cheese, and butter were items that I could add to their rations as an incentive. Another item that I was able to obtain was film for my camera. This item was not available on the island and if it was mailed from the states, you were lucky to receive it. I am not sure of the method used to make the film fit your personal camera; I guess there was a method to cut down the film to fit your cameras film size. I was also able to obtain the various chemicals needed to develop the exposed film that I had used to take pictures; I had constructed a small dark room in the supply storage building and during slack times on the night shift in the galley I would develop my pictures, and over time became quiet good at the project.

One of the perks, that were allowed in our unit (due to the nature of our squadron) was that every person in the unit was given the opportunity to earn extra pay. Depending upon your status, Aircrew men (the people that were part of the flight crews) were given 100% of their base pay while flying, ground crews, 50% of their base pay and anyone not attached to the aviation, cooks, bakers, etc were given 20%. The only requirement was that to receive this pay, you had to fly at least 2 hrs per month and many of the personnel never had much of a chance to do this, because of their work assignments.

"*The Flying Cook*"

With the hours that I had, it gave me lots of free time during the day, so I was able to fly (sometimes up to 4 or 5 hours a month). I can now make it known that a number of those flights I made were to locations that non-combat crews were not supposed have access to. If one of those flights had been shot down, or lost, some ones' fanny would have ended up in a sling. Now, back to the flight rations, being the night cook, I had the keys to the storeroom, and access to all food supplies (this included meat and eggs, when available) and some of the patrol aircraft were equipped with grills that had been made by crewmembers. This gave them the ability to prepare hot meals.

We had (at least during the first year and a half that I was there) to walk to the airstrip (which was less than a quarter of a mile from our unit) when we had the time to take a hop. During the period that I was making up the flight rations for the various patrol aircraft groups, I had became friendly with a few of the aircrews from those aircraft, and as a result could join them on a few of there patrols. Most of those flights, that were available, would be local test hops in SBD, TBM, SB2C, etc, but on a few occasions would make a patrol flight with VPB, 133 PV, Squadron's

I believe a policy was in effect that prohibited non-combat personal on Combat missions whenever they were secluded, but on one occasion I was on board during a raid to Wotje Atoll. A few days after this flight, I had a visit from the pilot of that aircraft, who informed me that I was not allowed to fly with his crew again. I found out later that his commanding officer had been informed of my presence aboard his plane, and had received a good chewing out about non-combat personal flying on such missions.

A few days after this incident, I was aboard another flight and after we had been flying for about an hour, the pilot called me forward to inform me that since this was a combat mission to Wake Island, they were to land at Eniwetok Island for refueling, and I was to be taken off and he arranged a return flight back to Roi for me. When I finally arrived back there, it was almost 6.30 in the evening, just in time for my night shift. Needless to say, this little incident would take care of any further air escapades on my behalf. Our main function was to send replacement aircraft, and maintain their systems, engine replacement, armor, guns, and the rest of their equipment, and ship to the forward advances of the war to replace lost or damaged aircraft, so there were always aircraft being flight-tested.

"The bakeshop on Roi-1944"

"The mess hall, on Roi-our dinning room, South Pacific style"

Bill Armstrong & Eddie Foster /1944Roi Namur Islands

Eddie Foster was one of the Bakers in CASU-F 20. We were about as close to being brothers as two people could be without being related to each other. We would sit around for hours remembering things that had happened to us during our years growing up, the environment that we grew up in was totally different. He was from the Southside of Chicago, a tough neighborhood in the early 1930's, and me from a totally different part of the country, Southern California, San Diego a small costal town of about seventy thousand, a Navy Town that was not very active until the War started. He had arrived on the island a couple of months before me, and had came from Majuro Island, a true tropical paradise; palm trees, wild and exotic animals, tropical fruits, cool tropical breezes, a real setting for a south seas movie.

"Walter Stepek- Fred Hansen-Billie Armstrong-Clinton Benson"

These three people were my Galley Buddies. From left to right, Walter Stepek, from Hudsonville, MI, who after the service, worked for Marathon Oil as a sales person, and became an excellent golfer; also became a teaching pro, until his death in 1995. In a kneeling position, Fred A. Hansen, from Wenatchee, WA. Returned to Washington state and worked about 2 months for the Boeing Company; then returned to California to Hollywood. He enrolled in dance school under the GI Bill and worked in Las Vegas on stage at several Casinos, then moved to Lake Tahoe where he became music and dance director at Frank Sinatra's Cal Neva Lodge and Casino. He became active in Hollywood and appeared in several movies in a dancers roll, "Oklahoma" in the 1950's and again in the 1960's movie "Can-Can" as a dancer. In the late 1980's he had a very bad stroke and was forced to retire from active dancing. I have learned of his death in April of this year 2005 in Palmdale, CA. Far right, Clinton L. Benson, From New Castle, IN, finished his hitch in the navy, then after being undecided and restless, enlisted in the Army. After his hitch was completed, he found work in the auto industry working in the truck body division of General Motors in Indiana. He passed away in 2003.

There were several young fellows in our same age group, and for the most part we were close, as we all worked under the same conditions. Eddie Foster had taken the late shift in the bakeshop (he was a Bkr3/c and was working the 12.00AM to 7or 8 AM, not too sure about the hours. We spent many hours talking, and playing ping-pong in the recreation hut (he was a good baker, but not too good at ping-pong). I still have memories of the many times at 2 or 3 in the morning when he would wake me, to give me a fresh roll, just dripping with butter. What a treat!

After being on the island a few months, and after a certain amount of time, you fell into a pattern of working your established duties, and boredom starts to work on a person. Most of the people find ways to cope. Finding some sort of diversion, a hobby like drawing, building game boards, toys, sports, baseball teams, horseshoes, gambling, which I found out to my sorrow that I was not very skilled at and stayed away from the games. There were a few individuals that were quite good at this enterprise, and gained quite a bankroll, although they had to be careful, as the amount of money that was sent home was closely watched, and that person was called to task before their division officer when they detected a pattern. The only answer was to pigeon hole their winnings. That meant finding a place to hide the loot, and more than one person had their money stolen. A few cases could amount to thousands of dollars.

Gambling was not allowed in the service, but was almost impossible to control, as long as the games were not too badly flaunted in front of the officers, because they were aware that this was going on and looked the other way as this kept the boredom to a minimum.

"Roi-Namur May-Tag"
" Washing, courtesy the winds of-Roi-Namur"

I am still amazed at the creative nature of my fellow shipmates. One such creation was a wind driven washing machine. Many huts had some sort of guttering installed, and this was used to collect rainwater, which was very soft, and used for washing water. We had no modern washing system; usually a concrete wash table and scrub brushes, this was all done outside the huts. This inspired a person to use a product that was almost always present on the reef

44

side of the island "wind" which was blowing 90% of the time. We used a 50 gallon drum and constructed a 2 or 3 bladed propeller, made from wood, with a crankshaft assembly driven by the wind, and would swivel into the direction it was blowing from. From the opposite end of the shaft, (with some sort of a plunger at the bottom, usually a can) all that was required was the addition of water, dirty clothes, and soap, and then away we go! A word of Caution, you had better not forget your clothes, and watch the wind speed, or else you could end up with a bunch of rags!

"Grand old opera, 2 AM"

A few of the crew members who were skilled in electronics were able to remove radios from wrecked or junked aircraft and with the knowledge, were able, (along with friends in the right places, bribery, and possibly a little cash) to convert them so that they could listen to state side music, and news along with this innovation came other problems that sometimes resulted in some form of physical violence (fisticuffs). The music stations from the states were broadcast about 2 AM in the morning (island time), which was disturbing those people trying to sleep, so you can see this was going to upset more than one person.

All showers were also out in the open air, not much privacy. Just a community affair with plenty of fresh air. If you were a shy person, well you either got over it, or took your shower at night. During the war, while I was on the Island, there would be USO shows from time to time, but unfortunately due to my working hours, I was not able to attend. I believe that I went to only one. One of the ways some of us used to pass the time was the hunting of small shells from the shallow waters inside the reef. By walking along and turning over some large coral rocks, you could find small shells clinging to the underside. We would gather them up to use in making strings of beads with small steel wire. The first thing that would take place was the burying of the shells in the sand for up to three weeks so organisms contained within the sand could consume that fleshy portion. When you removed these same shells, after this period, they were clean and ready to use, next the task of bending the wire to form a small loop to insert inside the cavity left after the creatures' insides were removed, cotton was then pushed inside to secure the wire loop; a very small double loop was formed by wrapping the wire around a small nail, then linking the ends together to form a link. One of the problems that occurred at times when you would turn over one of those larger coral rocks was what would come from under them. A very nasty moray, or conger eel, (nasty little fellows that if given a chance, could take a hunk out of your leg), so it paid to keep a sharp eye out for them.

"Fun and dangerous games"

In one of my previous articles, I had mentioned that there were many ways that crewmembers found to amuse themselves; one was fishing. There were the conventional methods, with hook and line, but there was also another method with the use of hand grenades. Let me explain! Behind the cooks and bakers' Quonset hut, was a small Japanese concrete round bunker, where they stored several cases of hand grenades. For one reason or another there was no lock on the door. Looking for something exciting to do, some person or persons, decided to play with a few of these marine firecrackers (remember many of these people were young boys) at that age, even in time of war, not all of their brain was working in a mature way. Someone suggested that they should venture out onto the reef, which extended about 100 yards before dropping off 3000 feet. There, they could drop the grenades into large openings in the reef. In this way the exploding grenades would be killing or stunning the fish. Unfortunately, most of the fish that came up were parrotfish that were not fit to eat and most of them had been carried out too far into deeper water, so we were not able to retrieve them. It was not very dangerous, until one of the young guys suggested playing catch with a live grenade, and most of us had beat a hasty retreat, but no one was injured.

"Midnight Lobster"

For anyone that has spent time in this part of the world, I am speaking of those full moonlit nights, when you were outside; it becomes so bright you could read a book by it. We had devised another method of fishing. It was on those nights when the moon was full and bright. We, in a pair of shorts, along with boon docker shoes (high top military shoes), would walk out on the reef while the tide was rising, and the water was about 1 to 1_ foot. At this time in the evening lobsters were coming over the reef to feed and with several helping, we could run them down. They always had to sit on the bottom for a split second in order to change directions and then you could drop your foot on them, grab and drop them in a gunnysack. As night cook, I would always have the copper (large cooking pot) full of boiling water; sometimes I would have 1 or 2 going at once and that, along with a couple of cold beers, made for a real nice seafood meal.

There were not many animals that survived on the island, after the invasion, just one or two dogs, I don't remember seeing any cats. What always seemed to survive were the rats and flies. I do believe that any creature that can swim, or fly, 3000 miles (nonstop) can endure almost anything. Speaking of rats, we really had some beauties. They were about half the size of a possum and looked somewhat like one, no furry covering, just a few thick hairs all over their bodies and boy these fellows were mean and you sure didn't want to corner one, or you had problems, I have never found another rat that looked, or acted like those creatures!

" ENDURING; Some did, others just survived"

Now that the war had moved ever forward, and life had in many ways, just became boring, the daily ritual for the larger groups filled their time between working and playing their games, hobbies and finding other ways to occupy their lives. There were also those few souls that had not been able to cope with this idleness. For one reason or another, their solution became alcohol, and ways to obtain these products, to escape from this island prison for a short time. The daily ration per person was two cans of beer each day, and you were given what they called a beer chit, which was a card with your name and date on it that you produced whenever you received your quota for the day. I was not aware of where sailors from other divisions acquired their liquor, but our division used the galley area as their point for this process. The beer was kept in the Galley area inside a locked refrigerator, and only one person had the keys. At the appointed time of day, usually about 4 PM in the afternoon, the process would begin. Each man would present his card for his two cans, and in turn his card would be stamped for the day. There were some people that did not drink and this knowledge was soon known and they became fair game as a source. The drinkers competed for this beverage, usually with money. There were other ways you could pay for this product like, exchanging favors, bartering for products, and services. I was not a drinker, but do admit to providing more than one product to produce an alcoholic beverage.

"Home brew, Roi-Namur style"

The knowledge that I had access to a long list of items that would produce something that was drinkable and contained alcohol soon had a financial and beneficial effect on my life. As the keeper of the stores, I was keeper of the treasury (since I was young and probably a little stupid) I should have been aware of the problems that this could cause me. As it turned out I was lucky, all that was required to make a brew was at my disposal; yeast, fruit, resin juices, sugar, and we used a simple way to produce the brew. Some how I was able to obtained a couple of 5-gallon water bottles, the type used for holding distilled water. I would mix the brew, fill the bottles, then find a small metal can or that type of container, punch a small series of holes in the top, wrap a light piece of cloth (maybe part of a sugar sack) over the opening to keep the bugs and flies out, then in the dead of night go find a remote location, away from the barracks, where the smell could not be detected, dig a large hole in the sand, with just the very tip of the bottle sticking out, then wait a couple of weeks. The warm sand and sun would do the rest. Later, again in the dark of the night, retrieve their loot, dump the whole mess into a clean sugar sack and squeeze into some form of container. It didn't smell very good, but had the desired results (made you drunk). When they ran out of liquid, some would eat the mash. Either way the results would be the same, drunk. A few other items that were also used as drinking items were, Aqua-Velva, an after shave tonic, which was 70% alcohol, and to drink this brew it had to be strained through several slices of bread to remove the wax and other less desirable product contained within, which if ingested, could really ruin your day. I only involved myself in this profession for a short period of time, as it became very time consuming and the fact that I was not a drinker probably led to my decision to abandon the role of bootlegger and the fear of being discovered probably aided in this decision. Another goodie was 90% alcohol and it was called torpedo juice, used as fuel for powering torpedoes engines; also used for cleaning gyro scopes (guidance systems in planes, torpedoes, and ships). There were other various methods to obtain alcohol (the real stuff), some was smuggled in by plane from Hawaii, some by ship, also much was obtained from various other units, especially Kwajalein Island, by various means.

"Keys to the Bank"

Because I was assigned the duty of night cook, which I have mentioned in other segments of this document, not only was I responsible for preparing the many items that were to be used in the next days meals and the flight rations for the next days' patrol squadrons meals, this gave me complete control of all food supplies inside the galley area, but also, full access to all items contained in the supplies Quonset, behind the cooking and baking facilities, which contained every item that was to be used in the cooking, and baking process. Numerous types of canned goods, sugar, yeast, and numerous and varied items that became bartering items for obtaining many items that one might need to make life a little more pleasurable and comfortable, along with helping the days go by a little faster. I was able to bargain for almost every thing that I might need for my comfort, and pleasure; film for my camera, items and chemicals for developing the many pictures that I took, extra batteries for my flashlight, items for making

48

shell necklaces, bracelets, and metals for other projects; also the use of a restored Japanese passenger car and a flatbed truck.

"Light at the End of the Tunnel"

As the war began to wind down in the pacific in late 1945, we began to have less and less traffic here in this part of the pacific, as the war had moved 2000 miles in front of us and less and less supplies came to our islands. We were having quite a large replacement of personnel (as many had been there since the invasion in 1943), so they had reached their rotation time (approximately 2 years) and we began to see many new faces. I was starting to lose many friends that had become close to me, and one of them was, Eddie Foster. I was to become a little depressed and sad about this. Due to our unit being reduced in size, I was forced to give up my night (gravy) job, because there was only a hand full of people compared to what had been here just a few months ago. I can recall that many of the new replacement people from the states were so interested in the war, and its trophies (souvenirs) from the war. A couple of fellow crew members, who were parachute riggers, repaired and packed them, decided that with a little energetic input they might be able to solve some of the shortages of Japanese souvenirs by removing panels from some of the older parachutes.

I believe that they were also aware of the financial rewards that were there to be had. They were able to print Japanese flags and sell them to the unsuspecting new arrivals, as the real article. I suppose they did quite well.

Early in December I received an increase in rank, to SC 2/C and was used mostly in a supervisory capacity; (whip cracker no hot grills or ovens). There was not much going on, due to the reduction of squadron personnel and in other ratings, for the most part, since the war had ended. No work was the order of the day, but every one still had to eat, so we had to keep working every day.

"South Pacific Junkyard"

Now, I need to talk about a subject that even today I was not able to rationalize. Shortly after the war ended, strange things began to happen! We started to observe barges being loaded with all forms of equipment, aircraft engines, some aircraft parts, wing assemblies; all parts new and used were taken in tow, past the opening in the reef into the very deep water, and then dumped. I was not one to complain, because it was not something that I should worry about, but even new items of clothing, flight jackets, flying gear (all those items were new) and still packaged and boxed. Many of us had concerns about this practice, and asked questions.   The replies that were given by a few of the officers in charge were; that the cost was too high to repackage these items and send them back to the states, because it was cheaper to make or re-manufacture and besides, all the ships available were needed for the transportation of the servicemen back to their loved ones at home.   The system works in strange ways; if you were to apply a system of numbers (adding all other bases), which would run into the thousands, you are speaking about many millions of dollars, but what did I know about this type of finance!   I was a little sailor, in a large navy!!

"Away we go, almost"

The first of January, I received my orders for transfer.   I said goodbye to the old galley and that would be the last of Roi Namur for me.   I was again sent across the atoll to Kwajalein Island to await my fate.   I had not a clue as to my destination.   In the navy every base or location is not given a name, instead it's a numbers game.   This is where the games began.   I arrived at the airstrip with my orders and was then placed aboard a NATS aircraft (Naval Air Transport Service).   I still did not have a clue where they were sending me.   They taxied down to the end of the airstrip, suddenly had a problem, and went back to the hanger.   There was no flight that day (blown engine).   Try again tomorrow!

Second day and away we go.   Finally find out I will be going to Eniwetok Island, (about 400 miles), so what's up?   A flight time of 3 _ hours, touch down, looks sparse, and deserted; surely this will not be my new home!   I must add this little bit of comment.   I was the only passenger on the plane.   VIP service.   I was loaded into a jeep, taken to a barracks complex, and dropped off.   Then to my surprise I was to discover I was the only occupant in the complex.   That's right, the only person there.   I was to spend the next week and a half, going to chow, movies at night, and generally just doing whatever came to my mind.

"Welcome to paradise, Majuro Atoll"

One morning I had returned to my Barracks, after having breakfast.
I was having a smoke on the front porch of the barracks, when I observed a jeep coming in my direction.   Inside was a Chief BOTS mate, along with an enlisted man.   The Chief said, as they came to a stop, "Are you SC2/C Billie Armstrong?"   "Yes," I said.   He said, "What the hell are you doing here? You're supposed to be on Majuro."   I answered, "This is where they dropped me off, told me to hold on to my papers and wait until someone picked me up, that there was only a numbered navy location to which I was being transferred, given no names, or locations.   As far as I 'm concerned, I believed they were sending

me back to the states." "Well," the Chief said, "we're taking you down to the harbor. They have a plane waiting and you're going to Majuro, so get your gear and let's go!" I retrieved my gear from the barracks, climbed aboard the jeep, and away we sped to the harbor. I was loaded aboard a Martin PV for my flight to Majuro and after being seated; I was surprised to see (once again) that I was the only passenger, _again_, a VIP flight! And what a noisy flight! I had never flown in an aircraft whose engines were this loud. Arriving at Majuro (it was at least 2 hours before my hearing returned to normal).

I must add this comment about the flight to Majuro Atoll. The view from 10.000 feet has to be the most beautiful that I have experienced. There was a cloudless sky and a view of 50 miles or more. The islands were green jewels, set in a never-ending deep blue sea, which is something to remember even today.

I was quite shocked after arriving on the island. The place was almost deserted and most of the Quonsets were unoccupied, or just a dozen or so people in some of them. I would hazard a guess that there was no more than 300 people total population on the Island itself. My Quonset was located on the reef side of the island, and what a beautiful location! There was a nice breeze blowing most of the time, and I must say Majuro was a tropical paradise, when compared with what I had been on before. There were palm trees galore and full of coconuts. This island had been spared the fire and hell of war, as the Japanese had vacated without firing a shot, leaving an almost virginal tropical world. Majuro islands' large and deep harbor had been used to form those large task forces that preceded the invasion of Roi Namur islands and Kwajalein. The islands' bakery supplied bread, and other items from their facility to the fleets and convoys being assembled at the anchorage. This is where my buddy, Eddy Foster, had worked prior to being sent to Roi. My Quonset had about 15 people there and there was not a problem of over crowding.

I was really saddened the first time I walked into the galley. This was the most primitive environment you could imagine; no steam cooking kettles, instead the food (or ingredients) was placed inside 20/30-gallon aluminum pots, a steam pipe was placed inside the pot, and a valve was opened. Then, you would try to regulate the amount of steam that was used. What a mess! I had not a clue as to how this method was to work (most of the time everything became either mush or soup) this place was just surviving.

Here I remained until about February 25, and then I was told to pack my gear. I was transported, along with about 25 sailors, to the airstrip, and then I was informed that I was going home!

"The merry go round"

The plane took off and we were told that we would be flown to Kwajalein for transportation home aboard ship. The next morning we boarded the U.S.S. President Jackson and that evening set sail; homeward bound (no such luck). We ended up back at Majuro 2 days later; there we stayed for 3 more days, until we had taken aboard more passengers, then finally homeward bound. God, what a mess!

I shall return!

"It would be 50 years before I saw my old buddy, Eddie Foster again"

This was some 50 years later; during a phone conversation with my old ww2 buddy Eddie Foster, the subject came up while going over the times spent on Roi Namur. I asked Eddie if the chance came about and we had an opportunity to take trip back in time to that tropical paradise, would he take the journey? This was his answer "I shall return." Those words spoken by a very famous man, and they also had to do with an island, only it was a much larger island, but an island nonetheless. Eddie Foster explains, "It will be 60 years this coming February since the U.S. Navy and Marines arrived in the Marshall Islands, and during those 60 years I was married, raised four children, who supplied me with eight grandchildren and a great grandson. I worked hard and had a normal family life. I played every game that used a ball and was a fishing nut; all in all I had a pretty good life, except for working in Chicago. Winter in Chicago is every month, but July and August. I hate cold weather. The family asked me several times, during those years, if I ever had a desire to return to the Marshall's or Gilbert's Islands, my answer was always a loud "NO." Time passed, arthritis and a broken leg, that wouldn't heal (along with old age) confined me to a wheelchair and now I had time to think...I started to live mentally in the past, and part of that past was in the Navy and the Islands. After Chicago's bitter winters, hot didn't seem so bad. In fact, it started to seem like I wasted a lot of years freezing instead of burning. I always liked the weather in the Islands until it came to sleeping in the daytime after working all night. There was almost always a breeze off the ocean that made working in the bakeshop almost bearable. Now I began to change my mind. Yeah...I would like to go back. I would like to visit Majuro, Roi and Eniwetok and have planes arriving during the afternoon rain. I would like to be there when the rain stopped and see if it was as I remembered it—the air washed clean and sweet, the sky was that beautiful blue. I want to look out at the blue green water and walk through the clean white sand, as I had done so many times, all those years ago. Most of all I want to see the changes. When I was there 1944, 45 and 46 all the occupied atolls consisted of, coral sand, tents, trucks, planes and men. There were no stores, shops, bars, restaurants or females!

I would like to walk the streets and just marvel at the changes. I would like to find a Marshall Island native who lived there during those years. I would ask about how life was under the Japan's rule. Was it better under us? I would ask how they made their living before WWII and how they make a living now. I would like to ask about their customs and their religion. As enlisted personnel, we were never allowed contact with the Marshal Island's people, so it would all be new to me. I would like to watch the teenagers to see if there are any differences from those in the states. Then, I would like to talk to some American servicemen or women and ask about how serving in the Marshall's is now. I'd ask about their living accommodations, their food and were their officers as chicken (a derogatory term describing the interactions between Commissioned Officers, and the enlisted man,) as ours were then. Today, 60 years later, I will say that in three and a half years in the Navy, I only met one officer that I would want for a friend or who I would live next door to. Then, I would like to sleep one more night there where it was air conditioned and see if I woke up feeling different than I did 60 years ago. Last, but not least, I would like to sit in a bar, order a drink and toast all the guys who served with me, then another one to all those who are no longer with us. After a few of those toasts, this no-drinking old man wouldn't care if his room were air-conditioned or not. Then, I would get back to my plane, ready to go back and resume my life, but yeah-I would love to be like General Mac and "return once more..."

Part # 2 the beginning, CASU F-20
November-1- 1943

On November 1, 1943 Aircraft Service Unit Twenty was commissioned at Alameda Naval Air Station, with Lt. Commander Vernon M. Williams, (VS), in command. On November 21 Twelve Officers and eighty-one men of CASU 20 were detached and ordered to Santa Rosa, California, for temporary duty. On the 21 of November, the first and second echelons of CASU 20 consisting of nine officers and four hundred, forty-eight men embarked aboard the U.S.S. KENMORE, destination Pearl Harbor, Oahu, T.H. After a joyful journey of some eleven days, the Officers and enlisted men arrived at Barbers Point on December 11 1943 for staging.

Photo # NH 98732   USS Kenmore in San Francisco Bay circa 1945-1946

"U.S.S. Kenmore-AK-221- Bound for Pearl Harbor Oahu, T.H- November 21, 1943"

The next day, they reported to Captain E.C Ewen, who was to be Island Commander at their final destination, ROI-NAMUR. Last minute preparations were begun immediately, and techniques involved in CASU functions were reviewed. Instruction was given on erection of pup tents, use of firearms, protection from bombs. Gas masks were issued, and part of the men were sent to EWA, for training, in the maintenance of F4U Corsair aircraft. Allowance lists and inventories were checked; shortages filled. One must remember that over seventy percent of this unit was made up of new recruits (out of boot camp, or a service school.) The rest of the group was made up with survivors of earlier actions in the war aboard ships, or from service prior to the start of WWII.

"The death squad"

In the latter days of December, a special unit was formed from volunteers that were given instructions and a few were issued side arms, along with basic survival pointers. Some of the others were issued non-automatic rifles, along with helmets and backpacks. This group would be used to help with the disposal of dead Japanese, in conjunction with the Marine forces on the Island. Two persons that had volunteered for this unit were, Harold Ragsdale AMM2/C and Joseph L. Niepozeski AMM3/c. On January 20 1944 this unit, under the command of Lt. Commander V.M, Williams, Lt. (jg) D.O. Hansen (sc), Ensign R.L. Watson, Ensign, R.C. Sherrick, and one hundred forty men, embarked in compliance with TASK GROUP 19.18 with orders, as the advance units for the invasion force, headed for the Marshall Islands and Roi-Namur. On January 21 1944 the remaining officers of 1st and 2nd echelons embarked in compliance with orders. The Officers being Lt. Newton Buckner, Lt. (jg) C. L. Brown, LT (jg) R.R. Cope, Ensign W.L. Prenn, Lt. R.F. Hegarty, Machinist R.Walke, Machinist, G.G. Reeves, and Chief Gunner, J.C. Rogers. Thus, began the journey, many anxious questions, fears, (scuttlebutt) of what was ahead? I must make a comment about sleeping arrangements aboard a Troop Transport Vessel. One thing they were not made for was comfort; no cruise ship cabins. With up to 1,500 or 2,000 personnel aboard at one time, the sleeping arrangements were sparse, to put it mildly. The lower _ of the ship is made up of bunks 5 and 6 high. Trying to sleep down there was almost impossible with almost no air circulation; at least not down in that part of the vessel. By the time air of any kind finds its way to that area, the flow is almost non-existence, and trying to sleep is a real problem, due to the amount of humanity, in such a confined area. Any movement will start you sweating, due to the warmth from so many bodies. Many of the Military Personnel, who could find space, went (above deck) and this can become very crowded, but from my own experiences, this was much more desired than the other alternative. Time passes slowly, as one day follows another and you pass the time as best you can by writing letters, playing cards, etc. Arriving offshore, during the bombardment, part of the body disposal unit, fifty men under the command of Lt. (jg) Don Hanson, went ashore to assist in the unloading of ammunition and on the day of February 1, 1944. The Marines secured the landing area at approximately, noontime. That same evening the rest of the Body Disposal Unit from CASU 20 went ashore to assist in ridding the Island of the dead and decaying bodies of the enemy.

This work went on for several days and it was during this time that Joseph L. NiepozeskiAMM3/C was shot and fatally wounded. He was to die from his wounds, inflicted by the enemy, aboard the U.S.S. Bolivar on February 3 1944. He was buried in the Marine Cemetery on Namur; his wound was the result of sorting out individual bunkers, in areas that the body disposal unit was recovering the dead Japanese troops. Harold Ragsdale's AMM2/C explanation about the actions states "we were working on a voluntarily basis and when it came to entering bunkers, to recover dead bodies, one person would take a piece of rope, and crawl into a bunker so as to tie one end to the corpse. When no one volunteered at this particular bunker, Niepozeski took it upon himself. He took the rope and entered the bunker, and no one really knew what actually happened inside that bunker, but apparently there was a Japanese soldier still surviving inside. A sad ending for such a brave sailor. In all the time, I had spent as an enlisted man in the US Navy, not one occasion had this type of incident occurred, to my knowledge, or I was not aware of any."

Harold Ragsdale, and Max Childs were involved in the removal, and burial of dead Japanese troops; this involved entering and inspecting Japanese bunkers, and removing the dead bodies as soon as possible, due to the rapid decomposition of them in the heat and humidity, there on the Island. This and the unloading of supplies was a sun up, to sun down job with not much time for rest. On or about the 6th, or 7th of February, Harold Ragsdale and Max Childs were down in a bunker looking for dead bodies, to remove and bury, when they discovered a large supply of Saki and numerous bottles of beer in quart bottles. They decided to remove a bottle or two to take back to their tent area. They had used a couple of canvas tent halves, to construct a sleeping area to share together, as there were no real sleeping areas setup, as yet. This sleeping arrangement was not a very large area, just enough room to lay down in and not much more. With the discovery of Saki, and Beer, they had taken back to their sleeping area, after another exhausting day. Max Childs decided he needed to explore their newfound liquid treasure and soon, due to the fatigue and liquor, fell into a deep sleep. Harold Ragsdale said that the liquor had no appeal to him and fell into a deep sleep. The Island has seen many alerts, since the invasion had started, so was not uncommon for some for them to be of false nature. Later that night, this was the scene, when an alert sounded, and due to their condition, Max, in a drunken state and Ragsdale, in a deep sleep of exhaustion, Lt. R.F. Hagarty and Chief Gunner J.C. Rogers, approached the two sleeping sailors. Due to the small size of their Tent, both men's feet were on the outside. L.T. Hagarty kicked the feet of Max, and there was no response, even after his verbal order to exit the tent, I suppose he became angry when there was no response from Ragsdale. So he reached down and grabbed the feet of Ragsdale and pulled him from his sleeping area. Ragsdale jumped up angrily and swung a mighty blow to the chin of Lt. R.F. Hagarty, rendering him unconscious, Chief, J. C. Rogers pulled a pistol and shoved it into the stomach of a startled Ragsdale, and said "one more move and I will shoot". He then marched him to a Marine Area, where he was placed under guard, until daylight, and then he took him to the local navy command center and explained the incident to the superior officer, who placed him under the control of a Marine with a rifle, who followed him around as he continued his work. A Court martial hearing was set with the Island Commander, Captain E.C. Ewen to try Ragsdale for striking an officer. A special board was convened, with Navy and Marine members. When Ragsdale was tried, he was asked to explain his action during this event, was told how serious the charges were against him and for him to give his version of what had transpired and why he should not be punished. Standing before the board he stated that his reaction was probably a defensive reaction, due to the stress, and strain of the times, that he had never had a problem with following orders from a superior officer, or enlisted man, and he only wished to do the job as best he could. After his testimony, the court-martial board adjourned to weight his statement and reach a decision. After approximately 45 minutes, Ragsdale was called back before the board and told of there decision. The Captain in charge told Ragsdale that the charges that he faced were of a very serious nature and the board, after reviewing the circumstances of the event, were recommending that he would be placed on a 90-day probationary period. If no further events took place, no further action would be taken against him. (A side note to this story, L.T. Hagarty had suffered a broken jaw as a result of the blow, and was sent back to P.H. for medical attention.)

Following the bombing of February 12 1944; a crew reduction was made and Ragsdale was shipped to Tarawa, in the Gilbert's, to help build a tank farm. On his return to Roi-Namur, some 2 months later, he asked for and received permission, to speak to Lt. Hagarty and express his deep regrets over the incident. He explained his wish that he would be able to leave this unfortunate experience behind him and get on with his navy life. Lt. Hagarty said he now understands the circumstances of his actions and holds no grudge.

"Here comes the Sea-Bee's! #1"

On February 1, the 121st Construction Battalion of Sea Bee's had came ashore with the first wave of Marines landing on Roi-Namur, as shore parties for combat teams. On February 2, on Roi - Namur had been mostly secured, despite strong counterattacks on Namur. The uprooting of all vegetation and the almost complete destruction of Japanese facilities, by the assault forces, resulted in a huge accumulation of debris. Before progress could be made in setting up camp and storage areas, beach development, or airfield construction, it was necessary for the 121st to remove this accumulation of debris as soon as possible. On February 5, the battalion was ordered to consolidate and begin their work to restore the airstrip on Roi Island. The 109th Battalion arrived the next day to assist with the project. The 121st, which was attached to Marine division, had only about 20 per cent of its equipment there, so the remainder of the project fell to the 109th. Of the three Japanese oil-surfaced airstrips, the runway that measured 300 by 4,300 feet was the first to be reconstructed. The existing strips were ripped up and resurfaced. The first fighter squadron arrived on February 12 and operated from the base as the construction continued. By the second week in February, most of the Marine division had departed and the remainder, with the 121st Battalion, was also ready to leave. February 12, Japanese Bombers launched a heavy attack against Roi; setting fire to a bomb dump, which resulted in the 109th, Battalion suffered 102 casualties and lost 75 % of its material and 35 % of its' equipment. The 121st's losses were; 55 casualties and equipment was transferred to 190th to replace losses from the bombing attack. (A sad commentary on the fortunes of war, as a result of the bombing attack in the early morning hours of February 12. The personal from both the 121, and 109th Battalions were not able to seek shelter from the resulting explosions at the bomb dump in the lagoon area, as they were denied access due to the location of the fire and resulting explosions; so their only option was to evacuate this area to the reef side of the Island, where they remained until the explosions subsided.
In the early light of dawn they started making their way back toward the camp area. Sadly a few members were taken, as possibly part of a Japanese counter-attack force, and in the confusion of the time, became casualties; either killed or wounded!

"Starting from scratch, part # 1"

"Marines of the 4TH division halt for a few minutes during mopping up operation to establish U. S. Occupation and control of Roi-Namur Islands in February, 1944"

The mess hall served its first hot meal on February 11, which consisted of powdered eggs, coffee, bread and pineapple. During the first week ashore, a part of the Engineering crew, along with the supply crew were busy un-crating tools and materials in the old burned out Japanese hanger, whose framework was still standing. Along the eastern edge of the airstrip, makeshift shops were constructed out of scrap material along with 16'x 16' tents. The work hours were from sun-up to sundown. There was so much material and supplies to move from ships to other areas. The hours were brutal and everyone was in an extreme state of exhaustion; rest and sleep were hard to come by, combined with the lack of proper food rations. Sanitary and personal hygiene were taking their toll, also.

The first aircraft to touch down on Roi, after the invasion, was on the evening of February 10. An Army B-24 damaged, by enemy gunfire during a raid on a neighboring Atoll, circled the field for a landing; although the strip was not completely surfaced. The Liberator landed safely; the first plane to land on the airstrip and serviced by crews from CASU 20 in the battle area. It was repaired and a few days' later, was returned to service. On the 11 of February, control of the island was transferred to Captain E. C. EWEN from Major General Harry SCHMIDT, and Forth Marine Division.

"Hell at Two Thirty, AM"

The only air attack in the Central Pacific by the enemy during the month, aside from attacks on our carrier forces, was made on Roi at 02.30 the morning of February 12. This attack was believed to have been made by 12-14 enemy seaplanes based at Ponope or Truk Island's. The planes were detected by radar at a distance of 100 miles flying at an estimated 14,000 to 22,000 feet. The entire atoll and ships in the harbor were alerted, and no aircraft were available to intercept the aircraft and the attack was very accurate and devastating.

"This night photograph was taken from a ship in the lagoon, shows the fires of the burning supplies on Roi after the air raid by Japanese bombers the early morning hours ofFebruary,12 1944"

A bomb dump in an old crater below ground level was hit. The blast disrupted radar and ground communications, flattened tents and temporary buildings, and started a number of fires. The use of "window"(thin strips of aluminum foil used, by enemy to confuse radar signals) was effective in preventing adequate fire control. Our anti-aircraft fire was ineffective and didn't destroy enemy aircraft, but as a result of this bombing raid, twenty-six men were killed and 130 were wounded.

An estimated 80% of the supplies were destroyed, 20% of the construction equipment was damaged, and two LCTs were burned out. Due to the rapid replenishment of supplies, no substantial delay in the development of the base resulted. The early morning moonlight was, I believe, somewhat instrumental in the success of the raid. It was so bright that you could read a book beneath it's light. Here, again, there are more disputes as to the amount and types of explosives used. Some say many bombs, others say a single bomb, and others said many flares along with bombs, whatever the answer, the destruction was complete and catastrophic.

"My personnel account Bruce L. Dickman"

61

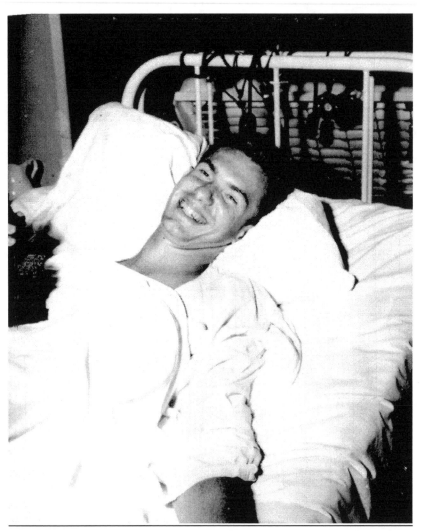

__"Bruce Dickman, recovering from injury from bomb fragment wound"__

WEIGHT 1092 GRAMS
OR 2 LBS. 6½ OZ

INCHES

___

"This is a picture of the bomb fragment removed from Bruce Dickman Back-February, 1944"

Bruce L. Dickman, AMM2/c was slowly brought out of a deep sleep with the sound of the air raid alarm; slowly he moved to his tent opening and slipped outside to observe what was happening. There was a terrific explosion and that was the last thing he remembered for some time. A large saucer shaped object, from the blast, (probably fragment from the bomb casing) had entered his back just below his left shoulder blade, just missing his spine. It severed the muscles, which controlled his arm and shoulder movement. He was one of those evacuated to the U.S.S. Bolivar and later sent to the Hospital in Hawaii for treatment and recovery, which required 15 months before he was to recover the use of his arm and other parts damaged. When he was wounded, due to the severity and nature of his wounds, he was discharged with a medical disability on May 20 1945. Bruce is self-employed farmer and has one stepson.

"My personnel account Lloyd Morene"

"Lloyd L. Norene 1943-Farragut, Idaho"

Lloyd Norene, S2/c at the time recalls, "I was in the third wave approaching Gold Beach in the Invasion force." He states "I was 17 years old at the time. The first of many jobs the navy volunteered me for would be burying the dead Japanese bodies. They gave me gloves, a rake, and a carbine with 300 rounds of ammunition. We buried 3,500 bodies in 3 days. If I hadn't learned to kill chickens, as a kid, I feel burying those dead bodies would have been very difficult for me. Later on, we had to dig up those bodies, because they had decided that was the place where the Mess Hall was going to be built. We were supposed to be given an Award for the good job that we had done, but to this day I am still waiting to receive mine!

When the bombing started early on the morning of February 12, I started running through the camp sight to the beach, where I laid flat, when the bomb exploded in the ammunition storage. The force propelled me about 8 feet into the air, and slammed me back onto the beach.

After the bombing we were mustered at the remains of a burned out hanger, a muster (a bringing together for a personal count) to define the number of persons missing, or wounded. Just then, a truck backfired and everyone scattered for cover. I was on the Islands of Roi-Namur for 2 months and I finally ended up on Majuro Island. It hadn't been ravaged by bombardment and bombing, because the Japanese evacuations of the Island at an earlier date, there was no resistance.

We used the supplies the Japanese had left when they moved off the Island. We had to pick weevils out of the bread and ate Spam off and on for two years and became sick of it.

Before this part of my story begins we return to where I had left off earlier and return to the invasion of the Marshall Islands. Since I had taken a course in electricity at Benson High School; I did the wiring for the campsite and hung wires from the palm trees. We used coke bottles for insulators, along with beer bottles. The first time we strung them up they shorted out, so we turned them around, rewired the camp sight and finally had this thing figured out (so much for a high school course in the art of electric wiring).

We were living in tents, at this time, and they finally finished with the construction of the Quonset huts for us and it became a cooler place to spend your time in. My next job was having batteries ready for the aircrafts 24-volt system. I made up Acid solutions and regenerated all of the batteries going into the aircraft. They had me on a telephone as a plane was landing with a 1000 lb bomb locked under the wing. I was supposed to hold the key down on the telephone and wait to see if the bomb would explode just in case there was a malfunction inside the planes' electrical system, which triggers the arming device. I guess they felt that I was expendable.

Admiral Harold came to Roi-Namur. He was in his own aircraft and onboard was several bottles of whiskey. While his crew was being fed, some one slipped aboard and stole the whiskey. We were awakened at 2:00am and they began searching our tents, looking for the whiskey.

Two weeks later, the liquor was being sold around the base for $5.00 per bottle. Whoever had stolen the hooch had taken one heck of a chance, but picked up a little change along the way.

I used to go along the beach and collect shells; I made necklaces and bracelets and sent them home to a pen pal in the states. Years later, I went to a thrift shop in the neighborhood and happened upon a necklace which I had made years before.

We took the crankshaft off a truck and used it to make a washing machine. We had two plungers fixed on the shaft, made out of buckets, and rigged it with a windmill on the end of the shaft, that supplied the power to drive the crankshaft, and move the buckets up and down. We had the first one on the Island, which was copied by a few other people.

One of the pilots wanted me to help him with the wiring of electricity to his tent, so he bartered with me. He had received several cans of grape juice from his wife, so I traded my work for his juice. He didn't know, at the time, that the cans contained whiskey. I got 3 cans of juice from him for wiring up his tent, and then he discovered that the cans had contained bourbon, "Why didn't you confide in me? I also earned money, giving haircuts.

My mother would send me packages and I shared them, when they arrived. The only time I was given a rating, was when I was instructing people how to install wiring and electric components, but still they were reluctant in giving me what I felt that I was entitled to, so I said to myself, I am going on strike and I didn't offer to help. As a result, they finally came forward and gave me a rating. They fed us Turkey for Christmas. It had webbed feet, so we weren't sure it was a Turkey.

Another job I had was driving a truck. One day they loaded beer on my truck, so my tent buddy and I stole the beer and buried it under the tent!

After the war, I learned the electrical motor rewinding business and worked at Tracy & Co. for seven years, Rhodes Refrigeration for one year, Standard Electric Motor Service for 20 years, and Tektronix Inc. for 12 years, retiring in July 1986. All of these places of employment were located in Portland, OR."

He was married to Julia Found in March 1947. They have three sons Mark, Curt, and John; also we have six grandchildren. A member of Anniversary Park Baptist Church, Lloyd enjoys gardening and traveling.

Harold R. Ragsdale

Harold Ragsdale, AMM2/C was occupying a hastily constructed
Fox hole shelter, with several other men, in the early morning hours of February
12 1944, when the first air raid alarm sounded.

Due to the stress and fatigue of the days of hard work related to the
invasion and not at all sure, in their minds, as to what was taking place when the
first explosion came with such force that the make shift roof collapsed down on
top of them. Somehow, Harold was finally able to free himself from the rubble
that had been their shelter, stunned and somewhat in a state of shock.   None of
the people, that had shared the shelter, had little more on their bodies than thin
shorts and a sleeveless top, not knowing just what way to go and with a confused
mind, Ragsdale started running toward the beach. It was a bright moonlit night
and as he ran he stumbled into the first bomb crater and due to the tremendous
amount of heat, generated by the bomb, he was not able to remain inside for
shelter. As a result he again got to his feet and stumbled out of the crater and

started running toward the beach, when another tremendous explosion lifted him up, ripping off most of his top cover, leaving only the collar around his neck and just a few threads remained where his shorts used to be.

After being lifted off the coral packed soil and slammed to the ground, he picked himself up and again staggered forward over a barricade and onto the beach. Rising to his feet, he noticed a marine approaching him screaming, "We are being invaded by the Japanese. Go over and grab that machine gun". Ragsdale looked at the machine gun, a 50 caliber on a mount, which was tipped on its side. Not able to right it, he then looked around and the Marine officer was gone. He remained there until the next morning. Staying behind the barricade as explosion after explosion rocked the Island for the remainder of the darkened morning. As morning finally lightens the sky, he was able to gaze at a horrible and almost total destruction, which had come over this bitterly contested slip of coral, here in the vast expanse of the south pacific!

A day or so after the Island had been secured, while walking among the wreckage and aftermath from the bombing and shelling, that had taken place during that period, Ragsdale and his fellow sailors came across a number of revetments, that had been constructed along the lagoon side of Roi Island. Inside those structures the Japanese had placed aircraft. These were placed as a form of protective insulations with elevated wall made from coral sand that offered some protection from the shelling, and bombing, produced by the invasion forces.

As they began to investigate the remains, that had been left inside those shelters, they were amazed to discover that one aircraft, a Mitsubishi Jukogyo, (Zero Fighter) had some how survived the holocaust that had proceeded the invasion, and subsequent fighting that had taken place to capture this Japanese base. A close inspection of the aircraft showed that the only visible damage to the craft was a single bullet hole in the tail assembly, and with this knowledge, they reported this information to the officer in charge of their group.

After a short conversation with several other officers, the first one returned to the group and informed them that they were to disassemble the aircraft, which at the time no tools were availed for this procedure, as it required special tool sizes (Metric). So they were a little puzzled as to how the were to proceed with this task, when one of the group shouted that they had discovered a complete tool set under the wing, near the landing gear. This set of tools was a complete one, so they set about reducing the aircraft into components, as they had been instructed to do. This would require several hours to accomplish, and at the end of this time, they carried this group of parts to the lagoon to be placed aboard a small barge and taken to a small landing craft, which in turn, transported them to a larger ship in the lagoon for transportation to unknown destination.

We leap ahead some 45 years to 1989; Harold and his wife Barbara would take a trip to the nations capitol (Washington DC.) where they would take a tour to the many interesting places that the nations capitol has to offer. One of those would be the Smithsonian Institute and Aircraft History Museum, which is located on the second floor. After arriving at the second floor aircraft exhibition, Harold was shocked to see a Japanese Zero suspended from the ceiling and this gave him a flash back some 45 years to the craft that they had taken apart at the time. He wondered to himself, "could this be the one?" After finding the curator, he posed this question to him. They looked for a serial number, but they found none. The Curator explained the possible reasons were that when the Military Services obtained enemy aircraft, in one form or another, they were used in flight simulation, with our own aircraft, to find out their capabilities when subjected to combat conditions, which will show where their weaknesses and strengths lay. During this process, they interchange parts to assemble more aircraft, from the many combination of parts, as was required to make a complete aircraft from the accumulation of those parts, as they were able to.

Harold M. Ragsdale was born in the Old Sleeper home in Ft. Gibson OK, on a very snowy day, December 2 1924. He was 24-inch, 12 pound plus baby. He attended Fort Gibson, first to eight grades. He went to Oklahoma High School, 9, 10, & 11 grades and graduated the 12 Grade at Ft. Gibson on May 15, 1942. He enlisted in the US Navy on May 20, 1942, received his boot camp training in San Diego, CA and was able to show some mechanical skills during testing, so he was sent to Aviation Mechanics' school in Chicago Il, and Detroit MI. After graduation, in October of that year, he was given the rating of 3rd Class Petty Officer and was sent to Corpus Christi, TX. He was stationed at the main base for months and then was assigned to Walton Field. He attended Aerial Gunnery School in Alice, Texas, traveled to San Francisco, Ca to Treasure Island Receiving Station for further assignment. From there, he was sent aboard a stinking cattle ship (USS Kenwood) for a 12-day trip to Hawaii and many of them became seasick. After arriving there, he was assigned to CASU F-20.

Harold returned to the states in December 1945, and was discharged from the service at Norman, OK on December 24, 1945. His first job, after the service, was training as an auto mechanic at Auto Parts and Machine in Muskogee, working up to shop superintendent. In 1950 he had an opportunity to attend the Oklahoma Highway Academy. He managed to get an appointment (1 out of 900), and graduated in July 1950. During that same year, he met Barbara Ann Boyd and they were married in December, of that year. From the union, came Shirley Jane and Harold Mack Ragsdale Jr. They are still married and after 20 years in the service of Oklahoma Highway Patrol he retired as, 1st Lt in July 1970.

"My personal Account by Harold E. Fulmer".
Harold E. Fulmer AOM3/c-Tinian Island-Marinas-1945!

Harold E. Fulmer, AOM3/c arrived on Roi-Namur a few days before the invasion. Here is his personal account: "Being in the burial detail for the Japanese dead, I went ashore on D-day + 1. It took one day to secure the airstrip that was on Roi and it took another two days to finish burying the dead Japanese soldiers. A large hole was bulldozed in the coral and the bodies were thrown into this large pit, then sprinkled with lime and the hole was again filled.

The next project was the off loading of ammunition, food, and the other supplies needed to make this island into a functional Military Base. A place was needed to cook and prepare food for the personnel that were beginning to occupy this island, and also to construct sanitary facilities (toilets, washing, and bathing areas). These next two weeks were spent unloading ammunition and supplies from the ships in the lagoon and storing them alongside the airstrip. The tents were erected along the runway, the ammunition was also stacked along the runway; I suppose this was done either in haste, or because of the closeness to the unloading beach, for whatever the reason, it would prove to be a very costly mistake. My tent was located about 50 feet from an approximate 20-foot high stockpile of 500 lb bombs. The Japanese were making surveillance flights from a distance daily and probably decided that there was a prize worth the taking. Sure enough they paid us a mid-night visit and the whole island was nearly wiped out in a matter of a few minutes. Most of the personnel were either killed or wounded during this attack. (In the final analysis only one person was actually a fatality during the attack, T. G. Towel ARM3/c). There were 29 personnel wounded and evacuated. The remaining 37 were treated on the island. The people thought it was useless to sandbag the foxhole, but at that moment I wish they had. My tents got blown into the foxhole and I said, "let's get out of here; we're too close to the ammo." We ran down the line about 100 feet and holed up in another small crater. Just then, the ammunition bomb dump exploded; a massive explosion caving the sides of the crater around us. I was facing the explosion and was knocked unconscious by the force of the blast and was buried up to my waist. Everyone that had been inside the crater with me had gotten out. I heard them talking, but couldn't move a muscle, they said, "He's dead, lets get out of here." After a short a short while (it seemed hours), a group of people from the harbor came by and almost dug me out, when the planes started making another run. They ran off, leaving one of my legs buried. I became anxious and fell onto my left side, injuring my knee rather severely.

I was sent to another island to recuperate at a Marine Base. After a month, I was returned to Roi. At the time of the bombing we had a couple of anti-aircraft guns and two searchlights that made a perfect target for the Japanese bombers.

After the bombing raid, the huge crater, left from the ammunition explosion partially filled with water. The people on the island thought this would be a great swimming pool. They didn't know that was where we had buried most of the Japanese dead. I tried to tell them about this, but they told me to mind my own business. After a few days, the bones from the decaying corpses began to protrude out from the banks of the bomb crater. That sure put a quick end to (ye old swimming hole) and the doctor condemned the place. Then it was filled with coral.

After about two months, I was transferred to Ellen Island in the Salomon's for the next year. It was supposed to be an aircraft repair unit, but the war was moving on so it was bypassed.

My next stop would be Titian Island. This was to become the main base for B-24 patrol planes, also the main base, from which the B-29 began their raids against Japan!

Tappan Stove Company employed me for four years, before starting a floral garden business, which he continues to own and operate.

"Frank Claiborne, Farragut, Idaho-July, 1943"
My Personal Experience

CASU-F-20 was commissioned an Alameda Naval Air Station in October 1943.
On November 21 we sailed under the Golden Gate Bridge to Barbers Point HI. We were given further training in December and part of January for our

participation in the invasion of the Marshall Islands, especially Roi-Namur.

Our convoy departed Pearl Harbor in mid-January. It was rumored that this was the largest convoy to leave Pearl Harbor since December 7, 1941. I was aboard a troop ship and we were told to have our helmet and life jackets close-by just in case an emergency arose. As we left the Hawaiian Islands, we were not sure exactly where we were going. Rumors and guesses were on everybody's mind at this time. The Invasion took place on January 31 through February 2, 1944. Some of the men were part of the burial detail, with the job of burying the dead enemy soldiers. I was not assigned to this unit, so I stayed aboard ship until February 11, 1944. Some of the men were brought in on February 11, checked in with our unit then were assigned to a tent we were going to live in. My friend Bruce Dickman from Silverton, Oregon was claiming my mail and brought it to me that evening. I was glad, because I received a great deal of it. There was a picture of my Mother in the mail, Mrs. Cynthia Claiborne, and a Bible from my Sister, Mrs. Nancy George. I was proud and happy to receive so much mail, particularly, those two items. At about 2.30 AM February 12, the air-raid siren went off and I was awakened. I put on my helmet and my outer shorts and one shoe, then I heard a swish of a big bomb falling; I hit the foxhole and stayed in for a while. I thought my legs had been blown off, then I felt my legs and they were still attached. I was so relieved! Everyone was running from the tents, since they had caught fire, due to the explosion and everything we owned was burning. The rest of the morning we were wandering around with what ever we were wearing. We were going toward the beach to get away from the fires and exploding ammunition. Many of CASU-20 were killed or injured on that fateful morning. We lived on a diet of K and C rations, for a period of time, and worked unloading food and other necessary gear. I stayed on Roi until May and was transferred to CASU-16 on Tarawa Island. I remember the first Memorial Service for those killed or wounded. During that time, two hymns that were sung at the services were "God will take care of you" and "Blessed Assurance," plus a Service which was directed by the Chaplains. During the bombing on the 12th, I noticed a splinter sticking out of my right arm, near the elbow. I pulled it out and later noticed there was a hole, so today I still have a remembrance of that day. Whenever I touch, or look at that spot, it returns to my mind, that early morning, so many years ago!

I was discharged from the Navy on Oct. 25, 1946. I then spent part of a year working as a mail clerk for the Missouri, Kansas, and Texas Railroad in Nevada, MO. I was a graduate from Southwest Baptist Collage in Bolivar, MO, Ouachuta Baptist University, Arkadelphia, AR, and served as minister from Sep. 1947 until retirement in November 1987. I was a pastor for 18 years and a denominational executive for 22 years, serving as an appointed Home Missionary-Southern Baptist Convention from September 1970 until November 1987 in Topeka, KS. Although retired, I continue, as pastor of Harmony Baptist Church near Appleton City, WI. My Wife, Ida Vee Driver and I were married on August 24, 1947, and have a daughter, Cynthia and two sons, Paul and Timothy, six grandchildren, and one great-grandchild.

"My personnel account by Clarence Hamilton"

Clarence Hamilton's rank was S2/C.

I was part of Acorn 21, a naval unit whose function was to set up the base such as; Radio, Cooks, Bakers, Personnel Offices, Mess Hall, Port Captain, (whose function controlled all unloading of supplies, also having control of ship movements incoming, or out going), from Barbers Point HI.

I came to Roi-Namur on the S.S. Robin Wently and came ashore mid-afternoon of February 11, 1944, and spent the rest of the day in a leisurely fashion. The crew responsible for the erection of the tents had finished and all of them were occupied. The work party had laid out several tents on the ground in preparation for being erected the following day. I threw my mattress and pillow on top of one of those tents, not set up yet, hit the sack relatively early, and went to sleep immediately, not knowing that I was very close to that huge Ammunition Dump. Suddenly, I was awakened by the sound of cannon fire and it was the Marine anti-aircraft batteries, which were firing. The air raid sirens were screaming and searchlights were sweeping the skies. I assumed this was a drill, so I rolled over and went back to sleep. The next thing I knew, I was rolling over and over with the tent wrapped around my body. I learned the hard way, that I had setup house keeping (too close) to the ammunition dump and the Japanese had scored a direct hit on it. I finally unwrapped myself from that tent and started looking around for a safe place to go. Finally, I dove into a foxhole which I was able to locate rather quickly, but was unable to locate my clothes, so I spent the rest of the night lying in that foxhole listening to the shrapnel from the exploding bombs in the ammunition dump, swishing overhead. I had really lucked out, due to the fact, that I had only sustained a ruptured eardrum. I would like to thank whoever dug that foxhole, in that unit, as it was my lifesaver. From then on, life was fairly pleasant. The weather was absolutely perfect and we watched a different movie every night (in addition to the base units, several of the other units had their own movies). I had a job in the Radio Shack, (a building where equipment was setup to receive radio messages.) I really enjoyed that; it was very easy. I was on Roi-Namur until December 1,

1945 and at that time, returned to the States".

Statement from Bill Armstrong

"I first met Clarence Hamilton, after the war, while in a service line at a Dodge dealership in Downey, CA, while we were waiting for them to open their doors for service. We started having a conversation on things in general, and finally discovered that we had been stationed at Roi-Namur with CASU-F-20 at the same time during the war in 1944-45. This was in 1988. We were to meet again later in the year with Ralph Rebich for lunch in Anaheim, CA. Clarence didn't have a telephone, but I received a post card from him on one or two occasions after that, but nothing since".

"Craig D. Carmichael,-1945-Roi Island "

"Craig D. Carmichael-My personal story"

Craig Carmichael ARM3/C I was a Navy radioman who landed behind the
4th. Division Marines on the morning of February 3, 1944 after Roi was secured.

I was part of a 40-man mobile radar team that set up our gear, on Roi, to warn of any approaching Japanese aircraft. The larger permanent radar equipment of Argus 21, were set up about a week to 10 days later, since they arrived on a different ship than the advanced radar team. Our equipment consisted of 4 mobile units, 1 radar van, 1 radio, 1 generator van, and a smaller open-topped trailers, with an auxiliary generator just in case we had a failure in the other unit. On February 3, 1944 at 10:00 hour, we were offloaded from the new 10,000 ton AKA 61; S.C.G.S. Aquarius in 4 LCVP's and pulled ashore by tracked diesel tractors, on the south beach of Roi, then hauled off the beach up to the edge of the airstrip. The grizzly sights and smells of wars devastation immediately greeted us, lying where they fell were hundreds of dead Japanese corpses strewn over the two hundred acres of the former Japanese airfield with its figure 4 landing strips. After lying in the hot tropical sun for two days the stench of the corpses, along with the smell of cordite and the acrid smell of smoke from burned buildings, and rotting vegetation, all in a sweet and sour foulness of odors. It is difficult to describe unless you have you've experienced it for yourself.

After waiting for an hour, in the blazing sun amidst the foul smell of the corpses on every side, we were finally hauled 300 yards farther inland to a position about the center of the island. There, we set up the equipment and were operating within a few hours. Around noon the next day, we picked up enemy surveillance aircraft at the extreme range of the radar and tracked them to within 5-10 miles of Roi-Namur. It became a regular daily occurrence at about noon and continued until night. In the early morning hours of February 12, at approximately 02:00 is when 10-12 Mavis flying boats from Truk, staged through Ponape. They hit us on a clear night in the light of a full moon, that you could read a newspaper by. In a matter of 15 minutes, from the wail of warning sirens, the deadly shish-shish of the first bombs plummeted to the earth and slammed with a thud into the coral island. In a millisecond, a hurricane blast erupted with a thunderclap of such force it lifted me up and slammed me down again, like a blow from a giant fist. That first horrendous blast came from a direct hit on the big bomb dump at the south edge of the Marine and Seabees bivouac area, where most of the 38 KIA (killed in action) and the 675 WIA (wounded in action) were, suffered.

The explosion of the other incendiaries dropped, were lost in that first big blast. In just a matter of a few minutes, the entire supply dump of 20-30 acres, were set ablaze, in a wall, that leaped upwards into the moonlit sky, and fed winds upward to the ten thousand foot level, then continued, until it twisted to the southwest by higher wind streams in a long black plume that stretched for miles.

My personnel account Fred E. Mainer" "

"Fred E. Mainer, Faragutt, Idaho-1943"

Fred E. Mainer AOM 3/c. "I landed at Roi Island with the third Wave at Red Beach. I was assigned, as a platoon leader, to assist in the removal of the dead; which were mostly Japanese. I was assigned to Carrier Aircraft Service Unit, CASU F 20, to take part in the construction of an airfield on Roi Island. I have saved many pictures, which I had taken, after the battle, to secure the Marshall Islands. This is a short summary of those events that happened in those days, during and after the fighting. Most were taken during February 1944, after the third day of the battle. The atoll was bombed for 30 days prior to the invasion.   We were part of Task Force #53, assembled in Hawaii. All ships, with guns, shelled Roi-Namur and Kwajalein Island for 3 days and nights; before we hit the beach   I departed from the troop ship, Bolivar, on a rope ladder to a L.C.I., and ended up about mid-ship. By the time we arrived at the beach, I was almost to the back bulkhead and I guess you might say I was somewhat frightened.   There was no heavy gunfire on the beach, but it increased as we approached the causeway to Namur Island, and we had lots of cleanup to do.   To show you how effective the prayers of my mother, father, and other relatives were, on the afternoon of February 11th our detachment was on an Island just off Namur, to perform work as a detail.   About dusk, the officer in charge saw a large amount of canned food. We had only K-Rations to eat since we had landed. The officer in charge of our work detail informed me and another sailor, that he would engage the security guard in conversation, so we could grab one of the cases of food.   Following orders; I took a case of canned milk, and the other sailor took a case of peaches. We really enjoyed the peaches, with cream. Later that evening, another event occurred.   I found a ready-made foxhole for the night. Then, In the middle of the night, the air-raid alarm sounded. This was nothing new, because this happened every night. We could hear the bombers coming over and soon the sky lit up over Roi-Namur islands. The sounds were loud, and the ground shook and trembled under us. Many prayers were uttered that night. The next morning we were up at sunrise and headed back to Roi-Namur Islands. As we approached the Island, I noticed there were massive amounts of 100 octane gasoline containers, which escaped the fury from the bombing.   You could only imagine the carnage that could have taken place, if a bomb had found this sight. Thank God none of them did!

When we arrived at Roi there was no sign of my tent, or my belongings, I had a large backpack in which there were many necessary items.   A few days later, I was walking through a bombed out aircraft hanger, when I saw a large stack of rifles and much to my amazement, there was my rifle, my name stenciled on the strap. I had no idea how it happened to be there. The Sea-Bees were busy repairing the airstrip and I was asked if I knew how to drive. I replied, "Yes, I can." I had only driven a model A ford for a short time, but you never say that you can't do something. They gave me a large flat bed truck and I wondered if I could do this. I'm glad it had a diagram of a 10-speed gearbox on the dash. As the days went by, the Sea-Bees were busy extending the runway (airstrip). We were very busy, with our duties, working on F6F, F4U, and SBD dive-bombers. In one incident, I was assigned to a gasoline truck. The air-raid alarm sounded and I headed to my assigned F6F plane. I was just able to stop that truck about six inches from the landing gear. Oh what a time the first few weeks, on Roi-Namur, turned out to be."

Fred Mainer was discharged from the navy on Dec. 8th 1945 after serving 2 years and 7 months, with the rate of A.O.M.2/c. He married Donna Bundy Aug. 30th 1947 and will have been married 59 years in Aug. 2006. He worked for Singer Sewing Machine in Centralia, IL as a sales person for 8 years; he purchased a grocery store in Walnut Hill, IL and was in business for 5 years, then returned to Singer, as a manager, for 2 years.   A friend started a Potato Chip Co. and he was hired, as a route salesman, in Belleville, IL. He lived there, for 3 years and then was promoted to Southern Division Manger in, Cape Girardeau, MO. He lived there for 6 years. Fred and Donna have 2 Daughters, and 6 Grandchildren.

"Harold Wagner on Roi-1944"
Harold Wagner AMM2/C -Remembrances of February 12 1944.

"We had several warnings, prior to the bombing, in the early morning on Feb 12, 1944. We had been instructed to prepare ourselves a good foxhole.

The Sea-bees, had put together a large row of tents, one against or almost touching the other with very little space between them, so I went about the task of digging my own foxhole and when I felt that there was sufficient depth to my project, (after sitting down inside, with my head well below ground level,) I stopped digging. I had come to the same conclusion regarding the placement of ammunition and supplies.

As we later learned, this was to come back to haunt the powers that be. Soon, an alarm sounded, and then 4 searchlights came on, one on each corner of the Island, forming a perfect target for the approaching bombers. Soon, two planes appeared, then I heard the sound of air rushing, trough the fins of the bombs, as they descended toward the ground. The first bomb landed between Namur and Roi, some where around the causeway. The second bomb struck right in the middle of all that ammunition, gasoline, bombs, etc. The noise and concussion was tremendous and ear shattering. After about 5 minutes, there were no more bombs, so people began to climb up out of their foxholes to look around. I came out from my foxhole and turned around to see what was happening. To my amazement all the tents were gone, and the remaining ones were on fire. I mean everything, that had been standing, either disappeared or was on fire. While I was in my foxhole, I was wishing that I had something, any thing to cover my self with, a sheet of paper anything. Due to the force of the exploding ammunition and bombs, I was buried, almost up to my neck, with loose sand and debris. I was able to extract myself, without a great deal of effort and stand outside my foxhole. As I was standing there, someone approached me, I could sense that; here was a person of some leadership quality, possibly an Officer or Chief. He shoved a rifle in my hands, along with a couple of clips of ammo and said "get yourself down to the beach," I walked out toward the beach (probably the reef side). Soon daylight began to appear and I could see that the sea was too rough, the waves were too high for anyone to attempt a landing and I decided to head back to where I had left my gear. The fire was still raging and burning fiercely. As I approached, I found that everything had been destroyed by the fire and explosion. Among all the rubble, I found my sea bag, and it had suffered severe damage, due to the fire. A fortunate set of events had come my way. When I was packing my sea bag, I had shoved a large galvanized bucket into the bottom of the bag and as a result, most of my personal gear was inside this bucket, but the heat from the fire had been so intense that what was inside was of little use to me. I remember one sailor, during the bombing, had walked over to one of the other Islands. This was possible at low tide and several weeks later his parents sent him a clipping, from the local newspaper, stating that he had been listed as missing in action. Shortly after the fires had subsided, and life calmed down some, there was a desperate need for clothing, of all kinds, as most of what the sailors had was lost in one way or the other, due to the bombing and fire. A call was forwarded to the ships, anchored in the harbor, asking for spare clothing that was not desperately needed, to please send it along for the needy.

We had no food, to speak of, so everyone was issued K-rations, a couple of energy bars, along with a couple of cigarettes. After a few weeks, possibly three, we started to receive C-rations, which in comparison was like steak and potatoes".

(I, Bill Armstrong) believe that, in other parts of this book, when speaking of the loss of materials, errors in judgment were made by the powers in charge, having the placement of all the materials in the one location.)

Harold T Wagner, after being transferred to first CASU 16 then to CASU 35, returned back to the United States, where he was discharged in January, of 1946. After he and his wife were married on July 5, 1948, they came to California on their honeymoon, and were so impressed they decided to remain. Harold took a position as an aircraft mechanic, with the navy, in the overhaul and repair department at the North Island Naval Air Station in San Diego, CA. He retired as branch supervisor in Production Division in June 1973, after 25 years of service. Harold and Jean have two children, Dennis and Shirley, and five grandchildren. His hobbies include woodworking and traveling in their RV. (Their longest trip was 11 months.)

" Bob Rittenhouse, Roi Island 1944
In Front of Sheet Metal Shop"

"My Personal Experience"

Bob Rittenhouse AM1/C. I came ashore on February 4, 1944, as part of the burial detail. Between the time of the invasion and the bombing on the 12^{Th,} as I remember, there were 2 air raid warnings, prior to the 12Th, when the main CASU came ashore. Tents were pitched (12'x12') and foxholes were dug in the coral. We did not have the benefit of sand bags in the dugouts and due to no enemy actions, during the first 2 alerts. There was a number of our group that did not use their dugouts on the 12Th. Quite a number of these people were injured, because they did't take shelter. Bob Jones and myself were in our dugouts, when the bombs were dropped. I was partially buried due to caving in. My head and right arm were exposed and Bob helped dig me out. When I was once again on my feet, we headed for the North Beach till dawn. That's about all I remember."

Bob Rittenhouse was born on Sept. 20, 1920. A graduate of Hershey Industrial School, in Hershey, PA. Rittenhouse served in the Navy from 1940-

46 and USNR from 1946-54.

He was stationed, while in the service, at Newport; RI, Pensacola, FL, Barbers Point, Hawaii, Roi-Namur, Norman, OK, and Alameda, CA.

While in the reserves, he was at Oakland, CA, Tulsa, OK, and Amarillo, TX, where he was discharged due to illness.

His last place of employment, before retiring in Jan.1, 1983 was as business manager for the International Union of Operating Engineers at Borger, TX, serving from 1962-83.

Bobs hobbies include finding CASU 20 members; rock hounding (flint-petrified wood) and working with mentally handicapped individuals. He has one son David and three grandchildren. He resides in Oak Park, OK.

"The aftermath"

As a result, of the bombing by Japanese forces, during the early morning hours of the 12th, there was a huge void among supplies and equipment, due to the close confinement area, where those items were assigned, added to the almost total losses that were inflected in this area.

I have spent a number of years going over official documents, reports, and personal accounts and I have come to the conclusion that this loss of life and materials, was something that could have been avoided, had the proper steps been taken and warning signs heeded. First, if the equipment and supplies had been dispersed over a larger area, fewer losses would have taken place among the items that remained, in a given area. I think, in an effort to unload equipment, and supplies, as fast as possible, probably was the reasoning behind this decision. Secondly, I know for a fact that the Japanese were sending scouting aircraft, almost every day, to access our progress during and after the invasion. I know this to a true and accurate statement, due to radar surveillances, and one of the personnel accounts of those times.

Craig Carmichael ARM3/C, tracked them outward from Roi-Namur Islands on the radarscope everyday, and yet no aircraft were dispatched to intercept them. As for protective air cover, none was provided. Why was this allowed to happen?

When the island was considered secured, major portions of the battle fleet were withdrawn; including air cover.

The day following the destructive attack of February 12, night fighter aircraft were sent to Roi. It seems that, once again, the resolve and tenacity of the enemy had been over looked. The history, from previous battles, should have been apparent, because their tactics involved night air raids.

We had sailed with these overwhelming forces into the western pacific bastion and seemed to have routed the enemy, but as we would find out, (in later engagements,) they would prove to be resourceful and a dangerous foe. I must say that, when you take the time to study what their bomber force was able to over come, in order to carry out this attack against Roi, you have to agree that to fly almost 1000 miles in total darkness, and carry out this mission was quite a feat. It seems that the military planners would again, in other situations, later in the war, continue to under estimate the capacity of the enemy to resist overwhelming odds, and inflect horrible casualties, among our service men!

Starting from scratch, there was an over whelming sense of, fear, anger, and just general confusion among most of the survivors, when the dawn of early morning finally arrived on Roi-Namur, that fateful morning. Smoke and dust covered the island, as the aftermath of the attack began to show itself. CASU'S Camp was completely destroyed and a large part of the equipment lost in the terrible fires and explosions that followed. The survivors had lost most of their personal effects, and were wearing what ever they had on, when the air raid started. Many were in their underwear, and most of the food supply had been lost, due to the bombing and the following fire, or it was buried under all the debris. Those first few days were quiet a struggle just to survive, not only were most of the food supplies lost, there was little, or no shelter to be had, as most or a majority of the tents, sleeping and mess tents were destroyed in the bombing. Fortunately only one CASU man was lost in this holocaust, T.G. TOWLE ARM3/C of Dallas, TX. Numerous other men, including Lt. (jg) Brown, Ensigns, Watson and Cope, and Chief Gunner Roger were wounded and evacuated to ships in the harbor. A total of 63 were wounded and of those, 29 were evacuated, A name-by-name listing will be found in the Appendices. What ever means possible that could be used to make some type of shelter for sleeping, and away from the elements was put to good use during those first days one of the biggest problems, was the lack of drinking water, all of the available water had been sent ashore in 50 gallon drums, and other containers, and as yet no facilities had been set up to evaporate fresh water from sea water. Another big problem was the lack of food, it turned out to be a very serious problem, since most, if not all canned food had been destroyed or damaged, exposure to fire and heat made the canned food unfit for consumption. So the only thing to do was to beg, barrow, or steal which ever it took to survive, for the next week to 10 days it was a fight to keep going. During the day material and equipment were salvaged, inventories taken and measures were immediately taken to secure replacements for those items that needed to be replaced. In the days that followed the CASU was assigned an area for their living space along the North Shore of Roi Island and the job of construction for the new camp could begin. Due to the lack of tents and lumber, the camp was crudely made out of salvaged bits of canvas, scrap lumber and even parts of airplanes a big moment in those early days was the procuring of an icebox in which a daily ration of beer was cooled for all hands. Shortly after this time, the CASU began to enjoy its first movies and athletic contests. On the 25 of February The Echelon, seven officers and forty-nine men, reported for duty.

"Return to normal operations"

During the latter part of February, temporary shops and working areas were completed and the servicing of aircraft could begin. The planes began to arrive by squadrons. VMSB 151, a Marine Dive Bomber Squadron, landed on March 1, 1944 to bomb and destroys equipment, and supplies on the enemy held atolls in the area. Then Scouting Squadron 52, another SBD outfit that had the job of maintaining daylight patrols around Kwajalein Atoll, followed them.

"144Crew 9#Tarawa-early VP –1944 The Feather Merchant's"

"Left to Right: Lt. Philip Horne PPC, Ens. Larry A. Moran-co-pilot, AOM3/c Samuel H. Grace, AMM2/c. R.C. Dalibert, ARM3/c Marvin E. Schandorff and AOM Samuel H. Hottovy"

"Under The Umbrella"VP-144-Arrives On Roi"

On March 30 VB 144 a squadron of 15 Medium Bombers, arrived for heavy strikes against enemy, held positions in the surrounding areas. All three of these outfits received their services from CASU 20. VP-144 was one of the air groups that had the responsibilities for the continued harassment and relentless pursuit of Japanese forces in the bypassed islands, in the Marshall and Gilbert Islands that had been bypassed after the conquest of the main objective bases formally held by the enemy forces, this included almost daily bombing, and also night actions against them as well. The Lockheed Ventura (PV-1) was well suited for the role that was used in, with a speed in excess 325 MPH, with 2 powerful Pratt and Whitney engines and they excelled in this role. This squadron with it's 15 plane group was to create havoc amongst those former Japanese bastions with there relentless attacks, and it was also to deny the Japanese the supplies that they desperately needed to continue there resistance (guns, ammunition, food, medical, and also communication with family) this they pursued with the utmost vigor. This duty was not performed without a fair amount of danger and sacrifice to both personnel and aircraft, although there were to be no aircraft lost to enemy action, still they were to pay a price in personal injury, along with considerable aircraft damage. None of the 15 aircraft in this group would escape without anti-aircraft damage, although we possessed complete control over all of the areas in both air, and sea the specter of death was with those crews on every mission, as the Japanese defenders, although out numbered were still able to inflict with deadly accuracy upon the aircraft that came within range of there defenses as they excelled in there response with anti-aircraft fire and they were deadly in there response. Operating among the Gilberts, and the Marshall, Island chain bypassed by the invasion forces leaping ahead in the pacific war they conducted continued air assaults from Nauru, in the Gilberts, Wotje, Toroa, Jaluit, and Taongi Atolls in the Marshall's and Kusaie, in the Caroline's.

"CASU-F-20 Commanding officer Vernon M. Williams and, Lt. Philip Horne Pilot fromVP-144- Pass a few minutes together as the find out the share the same hometown, Mora, Minnesota! –1944"

"Pilots at the controls during a mission with VP-144-1944"

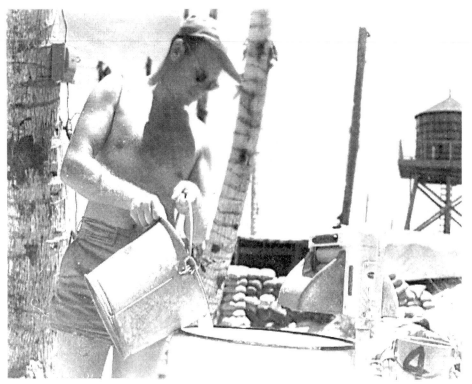

"Wash day with-VP-144-no Windmill needed, Ah, the privileges of rank"

"Nurau Island- during bombing-1944"

The squadron made 1,865 flights in the combat zones for a total of 6,903 hours in the air, and in eight months of active combat missions, in bombing attacks, photographic, patrol, and search missions. Only two trips were called off, both due to bad weather conditions. While bombing, and strafing enemy-held Islands were, by far, their most important asset. There was no real substitute for the performance of the Ventura's. As 18 of the six-man crews flew an average of 369.8 hours as VB-144 engaged in submarine searches, long tedious, tiring but again necessary operations against an enemy that would never stop trying to replace those items necessary to continue the war effort. Along with other missions, patrol searches, trips to disperse propaganda pamphlets, along with photographic, mission, and escort duty for big four-engine bombers on special bombing-missions, which were flown in every type of weather.

From April through June, strikes on Wotje were carried out in support of fighter and fighter-bomber groups of Marine Air Group (MAG-31) from Roi, and in addition, bombs were dropped on Jaluit every fourth day by four plane groups preceding between Roi and Tarawa, and in addition to those other sorties there were anti-submarine missions, along with special search, and destroy, fighter escorts, photo-reconnaissance and propaganda drops by the squadron.

Only on two occasions were flights canceled, and on both occasions this was due to weather conditions. It should be pointed out the flights were conducted during daylight, as well as night patrols, which seemed quite a feat. The squadron planes, on a patrol, destroyed two 200-250 ton inter-island coaster ships, while on patrol over Ailinglapalip Atoll, in the Marshall's, during the period from 19-22 January 1944.

On March, 12, a submarine was sighted and attacked by planes out of Tarawa, but due to the fact that the submarine was submerged, during the attack, it was impossible to determine the results of this attack, but on August 16 an enemy submarine was sighted 20 miles North of Kusaie, by the squadron on patrol. The plane was unable to close at high enough rate of speed to make a successful attack, and contact was not re-established despite deceptive maneuvers.

The only sighting of enemy in the air, by the squadron, occurred on January 18,when a bomber and four fighters were sighted south of Kwajalein by a patrol plane.

The only plane not accounted for, from this squadron, had been missing since February 14, when it failed to return from a night mission over Jaluit. Only one of the other aircraft, seriously damaged by AA fire was subsequently stricken from the records, had made a crash landing at Majuro.

Not to be forgotten, special recognition should be given to other pilots and their crews not mentioned before in this documentation, as they also, were part of the effort, and resolve shown by this air group, as follows! Lt. D.M. McAusland, USNR, sighted and attacked two armed picket ships on January 19 1945. The pilot and crews, prompt pursuit and subsequent attack damaged the vessels so badly, that they were later destroyed, due to their inability to maneuver away from the area, where the original attack had occurred.

The attack was carried out with only two 500# bombs, and in the face of intense AA fire, Lt. D.M. McNutt, USNR, landed his aircraft safely on Kwajalein, after his pilot was killed by AA fire over Wotje.

On the 19th of April 1944, the courage and skill shown by Lt. (jg) McNatt in taking control of the aircraft at, only 50 feet over the target and flying to Kwajalein, despite damaged controls and despite the fact that two of the crew were seriously wounded, points out the courage and determination of this group.

Lt. E.J. Rook, Jr., USNR, landed his plane safely, on Roi, after being hit twice by 20mm AA fire over Wotje on 16 May, he had a direct hit, by one shell on his starboard engine. Lt .E .J. Scarborough, USN, successfully landed his plane safely on Kwajalein on one engine, after receiving a direct hit on the one engine from AA fire over Jaluit, on 17 May 1944.

Lt. W, R Hayes, USNR, was successful in landing his plane on Majuro, after being struck twice by AA fire, over Jaluit on 24 1944, and in addition to wounding the second pilot, knocking out the elevator control cable, and having to fly 140 miles back to Roi and landing with only the remaining means of control, the elevator tab.!

Lt. G.T. King, USNR, made it possible, to rescue a downed Marine pilot and the crew of a wrecked Dumbo (PBY) flying boat (seaplane) near Wotje on June 27 1944.

Lt. King was on a photographic mission, during a fighter plane attack. He was asked to assist in the rescue of a downed fighter pilot, shot down by AA fire and drifting toward the enemy held Island of Wotje.

The PBY, in an attempt to land and evacuate the downed pilot, made a crash landing during this attempt at rescue; the pilot directed a rescue boat from a destroyer to the two rafts, despite the fact that the PV aircraft had reached a critical area of fuel remaining in its' tank rescued all the survivors and upon landing back on Roi, the aircraft had only 20 gallons of fuel left.

One aircraft, along with its crew of six, had been missing since 14 of February, when they failed to return from a night mission over Jaluit.

The aircraft, used by the squadron and built by the Lockheed (PV-1), had proven to be a well-constructed aircraft, durable and well suited for the tasks that it was being used for. It was equipped with two R-2800-31 engines, which when damaged by enemy AA-fire, in most cases, continued to perform, even for short periods of time.

The aircraft continued to fly their air patrols, as scheduled, under the most extreme conditions of weather, in daylight or on night missions. A great deal of credit must be given to maintenance and flight crews for the wonderful support in keeping the aircraft in flying shape, both in the air and on the ground. This dedication to their tasks, during their tour of duty while stationed with CASU-17 on Tarawa, in the Gilbert's and also, during their time with CASU-20, on Roi, in the Marshall's, the summary of statistics, during their operational tour in the forward combat area follows, and do believe them to be outstanding.

The squadron made 1,865 flights into the combat area, for a total of 6,903.2 hours in the air, and in eight months of active combat operations-bombing, photographic-reconnaissance, patrol and search missions, only two patrols were called off, and those were due to bad weather.

Bombing Sorties-338
Patrol Sorties-682

Special Scarches-42
AWS Hunter-Killer Operations-20
Photo Reconnaissance Missions-10
Propaganda Leaflets Missions-10
Escort Missions-158
Staging Flights-234
Local and Test Flights-353
Total Number of Flights-1865
Total Hours Flown-6903.2
Average Hours/Crew-18
Average Number Patrol Sorties/Crew-38
****

Personnel Killed in Action-6
Personnel Killed by AA-Fire-1
Personnel Seriously Wounded by Enemy AA-Fire-2
Personnel Slightly Wounded by Enemy AA-Fire-5
Planes Missing in Action-1
Planes Seriously Damaged by Enemy AA-Fire-7
Planes Slightly Damaged by Enemy AA-Fire-31
Planes Lost as a Result of Operational Errors-None.

" September 2,1944-VP-133Arrives "The Hit Parader's"

On September 2 1944 the first elements of VP-133 began to arrive in relief of VP-144, which would move forward to the advancing pace of the war in the pacific. Their duties were to continue to fly harassment and bombing missions against those remaining Islands, within their scope of operational range, still under the control of Japanese forces.

On the 13 of November 1944 Lt. Ward R. Tifft, along with Lt. Henry E. Lee and crew left on a long distance escort mission and the first leg would take them to Eniwetok Island for refueling, then on to Enebi Island where they would spend the night waiting for the arrival of Marine VMF Corsair fighter group for their bombing and strafing attack, against Japanese forces on the island of Ponape in the eastern Caroline's.

Ward states that their landing on Enebi Island was a little harrowing, due to the short length of the runway, which was only 3000 feet long and became a challenge to the larger twin-engine aircraft.

They had been instructed that upon arriving at their target, they were to remain at a higher altitude and just observe the attack and not be involved in any way, because they were to act as the mother hen with her chicks, as the navigator for the group back to Enebi.

This effort would require three days for this mission and would spend approximately 16.6 hours of flying time to complete. This groups assignment would be, the continuing harassment of those enemy bases on the still occupied atolls and islands in the Marshall's, also other areas still being controlled by the Japanese. Units from this group would continue operations from, October, until, March 1945 when they departed for the forward areas.

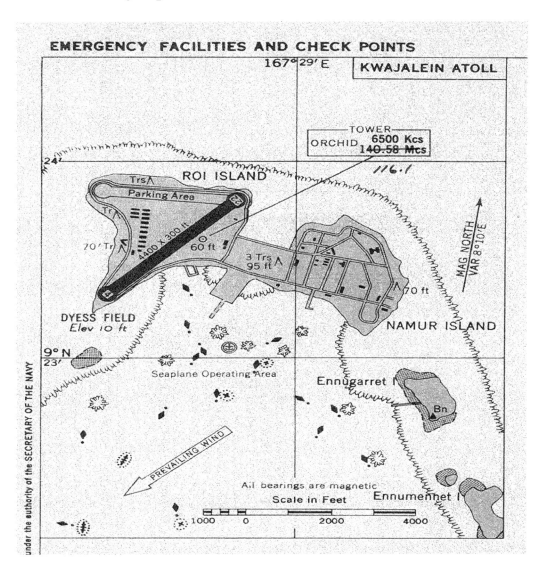

Roi Namur Island Map 1945

"Robert B. Allen AOM3/

Entries from the flight log of AOM3/c Robert B. Allen Sept. 10-1944 Strafed, and Harassed Kusaii Island, a building with a red cross emblem on the roof was noted, received some return AA-fire, but no
Damage.4.8 Hrs. Flight. Time.
Oct. 3-1944 Air Strike, Jaluit, received flack; piece blown out of my Turret, Scared S-less secured my gun and left my position-4.2 Hours Flight Time.
Oct.11-1944 Search Patrols nothing but water-4.8 Hours Flight Time.
Oct. 29-1944-Air Strike Wotje Island-4. -Hours Flight Time.
November 6-7-1944-Air strike Wotje island-7.7-Hours Flight Time.
November 11-1944- Jaluit Island, observed no damage -4.3Hours Flight.

Time.
November 27-1944- Jaluit, Island return engagement- 4.8 Hours Flight Time.
November 28-1944-Air Strike, Nauru Island-5.1-Hours Flight Time.
November 29-1944-Air Strike, Jaluit, becoming habit-4.5Hours Flight Time.
December 12-13-1944 Wotje, again, no rest for the wicked-8.6Hours   Flight Time.
December 19-1944 Air Strike at Maloclap Atoll, strafed buildings-3.5 Hours Flight Time.

January 13 1945. Five plane Air Strikes on Wake Island, led by Lt. Commander Elwin L. Chrisman, was a very long flight for this group, in this type of Aircraft.

Our group was up and airborne well before daylight. In order to maintain contact and fly, as a group, we were forced to seek a higher altitude, due to the heavy cloud cover at this lower area and finally at about 9,000 feet we broke out into a clear blue sky.

As we continued into our flight plan, it became clear, that the cloud cover was going to remain with us, so a decision was made to descend down through the clouds to a lower altitude, as we were fast approaching an area close to our target of Wake Island.

The weather this time of year is usually bad and due to the cloud cover, they were forced to drop down to approximately a thousand feet, in order to maintain their flight pattern with the rest of the air group. Once visibility was established, they were able to close up the formation for their bombing run.

As they approached the Island, intense AA fire greeted them.
The rear of one aircraft was riddled with shrapnel and machine gun fire. One of the aircraft's control cables was severed and voice radio disabled. One of the crewmembers, C. J. Zielazny had his helmet creased, and his nose and finger injured by the shrapnel, although his injuries were not serious.

"Wake Island-1/13/45-First Bombing Run"

One of the aircraft was having a problem with its fuel supply, as they had made a third bombing run on the Island and this extra attack brought about this dilemma.

The planes pilot, Lt. (jg.) Medard Z. Bryll realized their situation had become critical and decided they had to find a landing spot quickly.

Believing that returning to Eniwetok was not an option and with little remaining fuel, set their course toward the nearest large landmass that offered them some hope, Bikini Atoll, Taonga the largest of the land areas.

After just a few minutes, Lt. (jg.) Bryll realized their situation had now turned even more desperate and action needed to be taken.

He immediately started with a radio mayday emergency call and was able to make contact with rescue aircraft. Bryll was on his third pass, looking for a place to make a "belly landing when a PBM Mariner answered his call for help, telling him to land where he was, at the time.

The ditching was smooth, but wet. It was estimated the aircraft remained afloat for less than a minute, after they ditched. The life raft was quickly deployed and had only a 30-minute wait before being rescued.

"*Rescue At Sea-1/13/45*"

"Left-Right-Lt.(jg)Bryll-Ens .Johnson-Joslin -ARM-Hertz-AMM-Allen-AOM"
"Crew of PV-17"

After our rescue due to the size of the ocean swells, we wondered if LT. Goodman, the PBM pilot, would be able to takeoff, but after he ignited his JATO (Jet assisted takeoff unit) they were quickly airborne. Two hours later we were in the lagoon at Roi. Island.

__"Radio-Radar, repair and maintenance shop, Roi-Namur June,1944 "__

Around this time, the construction of permanent shops in the form of large Quonsets was well on its way. The first Quonset completed, would be used to house the Engineering Division.   In the next months, similar structures provided the Radio-Radar Division, the Supply Division, Ordnance and Aviation Equipment Divisions, with space and protection for their activities. The last large Quonset to be added, completed the following fall, was for the accessories shop.

About the first of April, work was started on a new camp, just east of the Argus area on the north shore of Roi, where a temporary camp had been set up. After the bombing, tents, heads, and showers for three hundred men were erected; this camp served as the permanent living area of CASU-20 and is only now being constructed at a site, one quarter of a mile west.

On March 5, 1944, a detachment of 15 officers and 487 men of the 95th Battalion arrived on Namur; their task was to construct an aviation supply depot, which was commissioned on June 10. Roi was strategically located for use, as a center to supply aviation materials for bombing missions against Japanese bases in the Marshall, and the Mariana's.

A considerable amount of materials and supplies from this base were used in the support of the Mariana's invasion and landings.

The 95th also erected a 4,000 barrel tank farm, with the necessary plumbing, and piping. They constructed hospital facilities, three dispensaries, with a bed capacity of 300. They also erected housing accommodations with floored tents, Quonset huts and barracks for other military uses.

There were a number of other construction projects that had to be resolved in the harbor. There was no deep waterfront in the area, so a small 4x30 pontoon pier was assembled.

A Japanese L-shaped pier, 450x33 feet, was used extensively to unload supplies from Small Craft Repair installations consisting of overhaul shops, for small-boat motors. Also 4x15 pontoons dry-dock with a 100-ton capacity for aircraft rescue boats, picket boats and LCM's was constructed.

A connecting causeway and a perimeter road for each island were also constructed.

Coral found on the islands was not of the proper quality for surfacing, due to the large percentage of coarse sand, which resisted binding; consequently coral for resurfacing was taken from the lagoon.

Native woods were used for minor construction, and native labor was employed in clean up and sanitation details.

In June 1944, CBMU 590 arrived to relieve the Construction Battalions and continue maintenance.

"To all who gave, we honor"

On April, 14 Commander William Mesek, relieved Commander Hunt as island Commander acting in that capacity at the end of the period covered by this history.

On April 16 purple hearts were awarded for those injured during the February 12th air attack, also on that day the airfield was named Dyess Field in honor of Lt. Col AquIlla Dyess USMC, who give his life while leading his troops, on Namur Island the second day battle.

<u>"Lieutenant Colonel Aquilla J. Dyess led the 24th Marines attack on Namur Island, the morning of the second day, while thus engaged he gave his life in this action, due to his disregard for his own safety"</u>

"He was awarded the Medal of Honor Posthumously, as a result of this heroic act. The airfield was named, Dyess Field, in his honor"

"Dyess, Field, Roi Island, 1944"

On April 23, The Forth Echelon, composed of 38 men, arrived for duty. On April 28, a decision had been reached; due to the heavy loss of material, and supplies from the bombing, on February 12, and the substantial loss of personnel from injuries inflicted during the bombing.

So at this time, a decision had been made to reduce the number of personal, within the CASU, to better serve the remainder of group with supplies on hand, until there had been sufficient time to replace the destroyed items and create an additional build up in these items.

As a result on May 14, two hundred men were detached for duty with CASU-16 and on same day it was also decided that one hundred and twenty men would be transferred to CASU-30 leaving CASU-20 with a complement of 17 officers and 181 men.

On the 15 of May 1944, was the commissioning date for Naval Air Base 835, which was commissioned and commanded by Captain E.C.Ewen.

Prior to that date, Captain Ewen was Island Commander, and had jurisdiction over CASU on all matters, particularly those involving flights of aircraft for general administrative purposes.

CASU-20 was under the command of Acorn 21, Commanded by Commander G.F.Chaplain, USNR who was under the island commander.

At the time NAB 825 was commissioned, Acorn 21 was decommissioned and its duties assumed by the new unit. Commander L.L. Hunt on July 11 1944 replaced then commanding officer, Captain Ewen, as air base Commander.

Since the commissioning NAB 825, CASU-20 has been under the island Commander for local regulations and policies. For certain technical phases of function as aircraft service unit, however, CASU has dealt directly with Commander Marshall's Gilbert Area and Com Air Pac.

"MAG-31-VMF-441 Marine Air Group"

Col. Charles A. Lindbergh Roi-Namur 1944-MAG-31

"The Lone Eagle Arrives"

I first flew the Corsair in July 1944 when VMF-462, a new fighter squadron was formed at MCAS EL Centro, California.

VMF-462 was deployed overseas in January 1945, as a replacement in (MAG-31) to Marine Fighting Squadrons VMF-441. I was ordered to VMF-441, as a replacement pilot during the period, February 1945 to June 1945. While on Roi-Namur in the Marshall Islands, we were involved in training missions, which included our introduction to aircraft rocket, bombing and strafing attacks against the bypassed Japanese islands. When we were briefed for dive-bombing missions, on Wotje Island, we were told not to go below 2,000 feet on our bombing missions, because the Japanese AA gunners were deadly, at this altitude.

Colonel Charles Lindbergh flew with VMF-441, as a technical advisor from United Aircraft, several months before my arrival.

Bill Armstrong states: "Charles Lindbergh was a very controversial figure, prior to WW2, for his so-called isolationist views, about the war in Europe believing that we, The United States should not in any way be involved in that conflict. But, he was not alone in his views, as the larger percent of the population in this country believed as he did, prior to the attack by the Japanese, on December 7, 1941 and he, along with the balance of the country, fell in line with the prospect of total war, with the rest of the free world."

The pilots, that flew with Lindbergh, said he was a very professional and precision pilot and after each mission landed with more remaining fuel than the other pilots. He also redesigned the Corsair bomb racks to carry a 2,000 bomb, on the centerline rack and a 1,000 bomb on each of the pylon racks, increasing the total carry capacity of 4,000, pounds.

One of the problems that the pilots had to face, in the Corsair, was the poor visibility from the canopy position due to angle of the aircraft to the ground, because of the clearance needed for the large four bladed props the plane was equipped with. This was later overcome with redesigning and moving the canopy back slightly, to improve the pilots view, and later able to perform from the larger aircraft carriers.

I believe (not enough credit) has been given to Charles Lindbergh, for his contributions toward the shortening of the war, due to his insight into the needs and the capabilities of the aircraft that he had at his disposal, Navy, Marines, and Army. His incredible ability, to analyze the potentials in performance from each aircraft, was amazing. He was able to pass this knowledge along to the young, and also older more experienced pilots. He was very methodical and left nothing to chance, in his methods, in regards to bringing out the best in each aircraft from the pilots point of view.

"The work continues and changes made"

The East, West Japanese runway, lately used as a storage area, was reconstructed by May 1944, with a new 2200-foot taxiway and a concrete parking area was also provided. The third Japanese runway was then resurfaced, for an additional repair and parking area, including fighters, light bombers, and patrol aircraft. Over 100 planes were now based on Roi. The field was commissioned on May 15, and from this base, daily missions were flown, against Japanese installations, on Wotje, Jaluit, and Truk

.

"2ⁿᵈ Lt. Elie G. Tremblay MAG-31- VMF-441 Marine Corsair Pilot"
WW II-Roi Island Marshall Islands

"Bringing Home The Palms"

On the 25 of May 1944, 2nd Lt. E.G. Tremblay states: "Our mission was to keep the Japanese-held, bypassed islands of Wotje, Jaluit, Maloelap and Nauru, out of operation. On that day, 11 of my squadron's pilots and I were briefed, on a plan, to carry out a low-level attack on Wotje, a heavily defended atoll, 100 nautical miles from our base. We took off before daylight, each plane armed with one 1,000-pound bomb, two 500-pound bombs, and 2400 rounds of 50-caliber ammunition.

During our preflight briefing, we were instructed to make our final attack approach, at low level, 50 to 100 feet above the ocean. The primary purpose of the mission was surprise, to find them unprepared, while they were in the process of making repairs to their damaged airstrip, other facilities and also, destroy repair equipment. After accomplishing our primary mission, we were directed to inflect more damage to the repaired runway and to find other targets of opportunity, with our remaining weapons. After takeoff, we rendezvoused with our flight in three, four-plane divisions, and headed toward our target with our operations officer, Capt Max Harper, in the lead. We climbed to 5,000 feet, test fired our guns and when we had flown about 75 miles, Max instructed us to purge our wing tanks. As a fireproofing measure, we manually, turned the valve on a carbon dioxide canister, which forces the gasoline fumes from the wing tanks. Following this procedure and to preserve the element of surprise, we descended to our lower attack altitude on the final 25 miles to our target, at 250 miles per hour at 100 feet above the water.

As we closed to within 10 miles, of the target, a visual signal was given to spread out the attack formation, which allowed for better maneuverability, while we strafed our target. As we approached the runway, we could see several trucks and other equipment, at work, repairing the landing strip. We flew straight down the runway, strafing the entire length. Our initial pass destroyed several pieces of equipment and their drivers. During the strafing run, we observed no ant-aircraft fire. We had taken them by surprise. Following our initial pass, we climbed to 8,000 feet, to commence our dive-bombing attack, dropping our 1,000-pound bomb and then our 500-poumders.

After each of us had made three runs, "Hunk" Nolan, the leader of the second four-plane division, called and said, he had observed, something on the beach, he wanted to investigate.

While we circled, at a safe distance, he flew a very low pass, parallel to the beach. I could see enemy tracers, from a concealed emplacement, located under the palm trees, on the edge of the lagoon, arching toward his plane. After Hunk had flown some distance, at this low level, his plane was hit, burst into flames and crashed on the beach. We made several additional passes through small-arms fire, near his burning plane, searching for Hunk; unfortunately, there was no indication that he had survived.

I told the other three members, of my division, that I was going after the gun emplacement, that I thought had shot down Hunk's plane; I began my high-speed approach, at water level, about a mile from the target. When I closed within 3,000 feet of my target, I opened fire with six-50-cal. Machine guns. Following my first burst, I observed pieces of the emplacement flying through the air. As I opened fire, with a second long burst, I became so focused on my second attack; I failed to notice how close we were to several palm trees, overhanging the lagoon. Finally, noticing the trees, I pulled up as quickly as I could, but was too late. My plane slammed trough the top of a palm tree. The impact was horrific, and I was certain the Corsair, had been fatally damaged. I called our flight leader, Capt Harper, reported what had happened, and told him, I might have to bail out or make an emergency water landing.

I flew toward a nearby friendly atoll, where a waiting PBY Dumbo rescue plane was available to pick me up. As I flew toward the site, Capt Harper told me the flight was low on fuel and was heading back to our base at Roi-Namur. Anxiously, I continued toward the rescue point, carefully monitoring my engine instruments. Surprisingly, the engine continued to operate normally. After locating and circling the rescue PBY for several minutes, I called the leader of a VMF-311 formation from Roi-Namur. They were just completing a follow-up raid on Wotje, and asked if I could join up for the return trip. During our flight home, the pilots of VMF-311 kept a good watch on my plane and me. I continued to monitor my engine instruments, which remained within normal operational limits. After what felt like an eternity, I sighted Roi-Namur. Receiving instructions to land first, I made a rather high approach in case my engine decided to quit; fortunately, the engine continued to operate normally, and I made a successful landing. As I taxied toward my squadron's area, I could see several of the linemen waiting. Apparently the word was out "Tremblay had hit a palm tree.''

After I had shut down my engine, the ground crewman began inspecting the plane, starting with the oil cooler intakes, which, on the Corsair, were embedded in the leading edge of each wing. I watched as they began pulling palm fronds out of the right-hand cooler intake. A work stand was pushed in front of the engine cowling, and within a few minutes, the linemen had removed bushels of palm fronds and branches from the oil cooler intake and engine cowling. My fellow pilots and I were in the habit of carrying a lot of material to Wotje, in the form of bomb and bullets, but this was the first any of us had anything, other than bullet holes, back from the enemy island!"

He continued to fly numerous missions against other Japanese held islands in the area; Wotje, Maleolap, Nauru, Jaluit and Mille. In 1945, he returned to the U.S. and became a flight instructor at Corpus Christi, Texas.

A year later he was discharged from active duty. Later, he became a reserve pilot in VMF-331. He resumed his studies in college, at the University of Virginia, and received his bachelor's degree, during his first year in law school.

He passed the Virginia Bar in 1950 and received his B.B.L. in June 1951.

In April, he was called back to active duty, during the Korean conflict and became a member of VMF-321 in Pusan, Korea.

After flying several missions against North Korea from K-1, Tremblay was transferred with VMF-321 to Kangnung, where the squadron flew close air support and interdiction missions.

During his tour in Korea, the then President, Sigmund Rhee, made Tremblay an honorary member of the Korean Bar, for his efforts in obtaining reparations for South Koreans whose property had been destroyed, due to un-intential friendly fire.

He returned to the United States in March, of 1952 and, once again, resumed his duties as flight instructor.

On 4 October 1953, Trembley was discharged from active duty and returned to Charlottesville VA, where he established a law practice in 1982. After having practiced law in Charlottesville, for 29 years, Trembley became a circuit judge in the 16th, Judicial Circuit Court of Virginia. He retired in 1990.

"Lt. Nick Mainiero! MAG-31- VMF-441"

Lt. Nick Mainiero, VMF-441 says, "I broke the cardinal Marine rule, never to volunteer," remembering back almost 60 years.

"On December 14 1944, the Squadron of Corsairs, from VMF, approached Wotje Island in the clouds, banked into a dive, and flew their bombing runs against the Japanese positions, then circled back to strafe targets of opportunity.

As Mainiero came in low and fast, with his plane's six 50-caliber machineguns blazing, an anti-aircraft shell exploded in his cockpit, blowing off his canopy, knocking out his instruments and flight controls, then sliced his arms, shoulders and face with shrapnel. With the guidance of his wingman, Mainiero flew his damaged plane back to Kwajalein Atoll, in the Marshall Islands and landed safely.

"At the time, I didn't know there was anything wrong," said Hugh Pickering, another young Marine lieutenant in VMF-441, who watched Mainiero land.

On another mission in 1944, an anti-aircraft shell blew almost all of his Corsair's entire vertical tail stabilizer.

"Nick Mainiero, standing beside his damaged aircraft, back on Roi"

Without a rudder, it was extremely difficult to keep the aircraft in the air, but Mainiero managed to control the aircraft, then managed to fly the remaining 200 miles back to his base and land safely.

He remarks, that when the aircraft is in top shape, flying a Corsair was like driving a Cadillac; it trimmed up perfectly, and was a joy to fly!
Mainiero, on his last combat mission lost an eye. As a 21-year-old Second Lieutenant; Mainiero scored a direct hit with a 500-pound bomb, on a munitions storage facility, on the Island of Wotje. During the dive, to drop the bomb, a 20-mm anti-aircraft shell, struck his cockpit, and as a result, he received a severe injury to his to head. The resulting consequence was the loss of an eye.

The rudder of his plane was shot away, but Mainiero was able to return to his land base. He didn't pass out, until after he landed safely.

As a result of this action, he was awarded the Distinguished Flying Cross and Purple Heart. Because of his eye loss, Mianiero lost his ability to remain as a pilot.

After retiring, he took the position as manager of the Sikorsky Memorial Airport. He is retired, from that position, and spends a large portion of his time in Florida, where he plays a little golf.

Irwin's experience, flying with Air Group, 14 VMF-251. In April 1945, he was making an air strike, against the Japanese, in Cebu City in the Philippines, when one of his 500-pound bombs, he was carrying, refused to release from it's mounting rack, under the plane. No matter what action he tried, he was not able to release it from the rack.

He couldn't shake it loose, no matter what he had tried, but when his plane touched down, on the runway, the bomb detached itself. The bomb's safety devices malfunctioned and exploded beneath his plane. It demolished the aircraft, behind the armored cockpit, but he walked away, with only minor shrapnel wounds.

"Lt. George Diemier Jr. MAG-31-VMF-331"

Lt. George Diemier, was from Warrensburg, MO. A graduate of Central Missouri State Teachers College in 1940, where his father was the President.

He and his brother organized a dance band, while in college, which they kept together for a couple of years. He was a talented musician, and accomplished pianist and cornet player, with a fine baritone voice. While stationed at Olathe air Base in Kansas he was their bugler and carried the instrument with him, wherever he went.

He was a high school teacher for a couple of years, and then joined the Marines in the summer of 1942. After training, with the Marines at Pensacola, Miami, Norfolk and Parris Island, he was sent to the South Pacific to Wallis Island, in the Samoa Group in September, 1943.

From there they were transported as part of the invasion forces, which were to take part in the invasion of the Marshall Islands, Kwajalein Atoll and Roi-Namur. After the invasion, and when the Islands were secured, they went ashore on February 10 1944, to set up their quarters.

"We had just got settled, when we received our first reminder that the Japanese were still in the area. At 2: 15AM, our second night here on Roi, an alert sounded. I hurriedly, grabbed my trousers; shoes and helmet, then took off running, along with several other officers, to a battered, but sound Japanese, pillbox. We were joking among ourselves, when we heard a swish and felt the most tremendous concussion of our lives. We were all lifted several feet into the air and my helmet flew across the pillbox. I fervently hope, that I never have to experience such an awful feeling that first bomb gave me.

It was a mingling of incredible, fear, helplessness and confusion. Immediately I started to working on my state of mind; praying being my chief tool and soon, several of us began to talk among ourselves and even joked among us.

The next few hours were as close to predation as I ever care to come, but after my first attack of hopelessness, I managed to keep a firm hold upon my reasoning and faith.

I soon learned that, religion was far from dead, and that first bomb awakened the soul of every man to awareness and need of divine power. Shortly after 6:00AM, we eased out of the pillbox, only to discover that actually we had taken shelter in an ammunition bunker! I had been kneeling on a 5-inch shell!

When we arrived at our campsite it was awfully barren; where once had been our tents and beds, there now remained only ashes.

The first bomb had wiped out the officers' area. I looked vainly for my belongings, and was almost heartbroken, by the strangely misshapen mess that had once been Connie. (His Coronet)''

"In another letter he wrote home"

"My next home was a foxhole on the beach.... I had no bedding and the nights there were actually cold, with a strong ocean breeze blowing constantly.

Bill Fuller and I dug a 2-man foxhole and lined it with sand bags; we managed to make it quite homey.

The next day we found a blanket and a few more clothes. That night turned out to be a little more comfortable, although the tide threatened to wash us out. I have now earned full privileges, at the Beach club…Of course; it was a laundry, bathing, and swimming pool; coincidentally, located in the same spot, The Ocean."

The Warrensburg Star-Journal article describes how his family was notified of his death:

Lt. George W. Diemer, Jr. US Marine Corps Reserve, was killed in an aircraft crash in the South Pacific area. President and Mrs. George W. Diemer, of the College, were notified Tuesday, by the War Department. Lt Diemer was 23 years old at the time of his death!

"50 Years later-Finalizing Closure through e-mails-Amazing what technology does nowadays"

From Craig Carmichael! "I was a witness to the incident, in which Lt. Diemer was drowned on Roi-Namur. When his plane crashed, during takeoff at the far end of the runway, on the reef and into the water, during high tide. Lt. Diemer made a fatal error when he left his cockpit, and this decision would lead to his death. He had climbed out onto the wing and somehow, slipped into the dangerous undertow, that pulled him down, and probably raked him against the jagged coral, which was razor sharp and was drowned, when rescue was just a few moments away, as a rescue boat was coming into view, around the north point of Namur, while he was there

We had been on our way to chow on a flat bed truck, which was halted by an SP at the end of the runway, and witnessed the F-4U Corsair, in the shallow water, on the reef; about 100 yards from the end of the runway.

While we watched, the pilot leave the safety of the cockpit, and climb out on the wing, which was barely out of reach of the waves, from the incoming tide. We didn't see him slip and fall from the wing, but heard about it on our way back from the chow hall. It's another one of those incidents that could have been averted, with a little more caution and was a sad ending to a young mans' life and flying career. Flying is always surrounded with risks; in training and in combat!"

"And The Beat Goes On"

In July 1944, CASU started receiving damaged aircraft, from the fleet in need of repairs or for salvage. In August, a plane pool was informally started. It was actually made of a sub-division of the Engineering Department.

On November 22 1944, the accommodation of all men wishing to exercise their voting privileges, through the use of the War Ballot, was begun on the 12 of August by Lt. H.E. Eiffert, voting officer, and was carried out, according to the rules set forth.

A detachment of two officers, and fifty men, from PATSU 26, arrived on August 15 for temporary duty, to assist in the salvage operations at the Plane Pool; they completed their work and were detached 11 days later.

A squadron of 15 Medium PV Bombers arrived on 2 September, to relieve VP 144 and continue with air strikes against Japanese held atolls in the area. The new squadron was VB 133.

In the months that followed, CASU's main duties involved servicing and repairing the planes of VB 133, and Scouting Squadron 52. There were also other duties regularly assigned to the CASU repair and service unit.

A repair to transit aircraft, Staff aircraft was attached to Commander Marshall's Gilbert area. CASU also did considerable work, and service, to planes attached to Marine Squadrons; especially those attached to Marine Air Group 31, which was striking the enemy, in those areas still occupied within striking range and getting ready to move forward with the war!

"Expansion of the war against the enemy"

The Accessory and Overhaul shops were erected in the fall of 1944 and placed into operation in October. The Plane Pool was to expand, during this period, assuming the job of preserving and de-preserving aircraft; largely for the needs of the Marshall Gilberts Area. By November of 1944, life in CASU-20 had settled down to a regular routine. The bulk, of the building programs, had been accomplished,

Various local problems, arising from limited facilities, had been resolved and operating Squadrons serviced, without any difficulty.

The complement of CASU members, about 600, remained the same for the next six months. On the seventh of April 1945, VB 133 left the island for an advanced area, and operations began to decline.

The work of CASU-20 slackened accordingly, and for the first time since coming to Roi Island, the crews were given Sundays off, with maintenance work being carried on, by a watch section.

Recreation and athletic activities were greatly expanded, an excellent athletic area built, picnic arranged, a beer garden of thatch construction put up, and other devices, to keep up the morale, increased.

A weekly newspaper made its appearance for the first time. Those welfare and athletic programs were in addition to regular standbys; such as movies and beer, which the men had enjoyed from the beginning on ROI.

Commander Vernon M. Williams, who had engineered CASU's destiny from it's inception, through its' trial period in the early days and a routine era, was relieved on May 28 by, Lt. Commander Henry W. Fish, S (A), USNR. He resumed command, at an inspection ceremony, on the apron in front of shop area.

Three days later, on May 31, VS 52 was detached from ROI and was replaced, that day, by a section of six planes from VS 66, which is currently maintaining patrols and anti-submarine flights over Kwajalein Atoll.

With the departure of two main squadrons and their replacement with six Scouting Planes, it was expected, in June that the work of CASU 20 was practically over. This opinion was short-lived, for in the middle of June, word was received; the activities on ROI were to be expanded, especially the work in the Plane Pool.

To prepare for this load, plans were drawn up for expansion of the shop, and pool, facilities and living quarters, for the men. By the end of June, the plans were already taking shape, in a larger building program, to double CASU's output.

"B-29 on Roi 1945"

In early 1945, this B-29 Super Fortress had developed mechanical problems, and because of this, was not able to reach the longer runway on Kwajalein Island, so was forced to use the shorter air strip on Roi Island, where it was to stay for a few days, until that problem was resolved.

As a result, most of the equipment, which could be removed from that aircraft, was off loaded to lighten the plane, so they could become airborne from our shorter runway. Thus, they were able to accomplish this feat, but it took every inch of this airstrip to do so.

Their guns, and other equipment were taken, by boat, to their location on Kwajalien Island.

"Changing of the Guard"

During the latter months of 1945, CASU was experiencing a rapid influx of replacement personal to fill the void left, due to rotations, of personnel, back to the US for reassignment and RR, (rest and relaxation).

Many of the new personal had no prior over seas duty, or were new recruits, fresh out of basic training. Quite a large number had been stationed for the greater portion, of their naval service at one or more naval facilities, in the United States. At this time, they were sent over seas to give them a more balanced service time, which in some respects was the only fair way to even out overseas assignment times for all individuals in this conflict, during their enlistment.

As the war wound down and finally came to an end, activities there on Roi-Namur were fast approaching. They were ending, as far as war related duties were concerned. Repair and maintenance, had almost come to a halt, as repair and servicing of aircraft had slowed to almost nothing and so many of the higher rated and skilled personnel had been sent home. Their overseas time had earned them that privilege.

"Flags, and Travel Luggage"

"I must make a comment here, about the arrival of so many new replacement personnel that had been arriving, a short time, before the ending of hostilities and after. Most of them had no previous duty overseas; in fact they were 17-18 year old new recruits, and looking for some type of war souvenirs to obtain for their memories of this time in history. They were those individuals, here on Roi-Namur that saw an opportunity to cash in on this bonanza.

The biggest reward would be to obtain a Japanese battle flag to show the folks back home, now the problem was that any flags of that nature had long sense been removed.

Now a person, or persons with access to materials, could very easily be made into those objects of high demand; namely, people (parachute riggers) in the parachute maintenance building, where they were housed for storage and repair, jumped into the flag making business.

By removing panels, from worn or defective chutes, they began the production of those items. They were cut to size, a method of printing was set up and money exchanged hands. Another item that was also produced and sold as luggage, or what might be called luggage, (I know this to be a fact, as I myself, purchased one of those items of luggage.) I believe they were called Parachute Bags.

On the 18, of January 1946, I received my orders for transfer. There were now just a handful of personnel left, in our unit, which included Supply, Commissary, Cooks and Bakers. I was instructed to close up the Galley and Bakery, which I did and that would be the last meal, or loaf of bread, from that unit. As I had locked the doors, and took the keys with me, if any one used the Galley or other parts of the building, after my departure, I can't be sure, because I retained the keys, and they are still in my possession.

I don't believe this was possible, because there were no cooks or bakers left in CASU-20, as I was the last man out of <u>Dodge!</u>"

<u>"The Aftermath, The end of the struggle (Victory)"</u>

Following Japan's acceptances of Allied terms, the first overseas Japanese post to surrender was at Mile Atoll, in the Southeastern Marshall Islands. One of several "bypassed" island garrisons, in the Central Pacific,

Photo # 80-G-490368 Capt. Shiga boards USS Levy, off Mille Atoll, 22 August 1945

Japanese Navy Captain, Masanori Shiga gives his salute, as he comes aboard the USS Levy (DE-16) of Mille Atoll, of the Marshall's Island Group, as he prepares to surrender, the former Japanese base here on August 22, 1945."

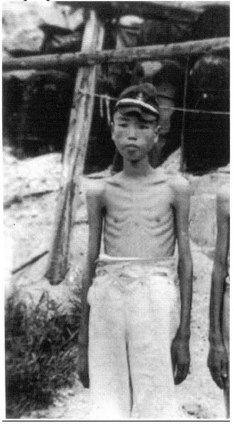

"Japanese survivor from Wotje Island"

"Standing Proud, but Starving"

Photo # 80-G-490369 Signing surrender of Mille Atoll, 22 August 1945

Marine officer, BRIGADIER GENERAL L. H. M USMC, Received the
Surrender of Wake Island By Japanese, September 4 1945
Island surrender from Admiral Sakaibara.

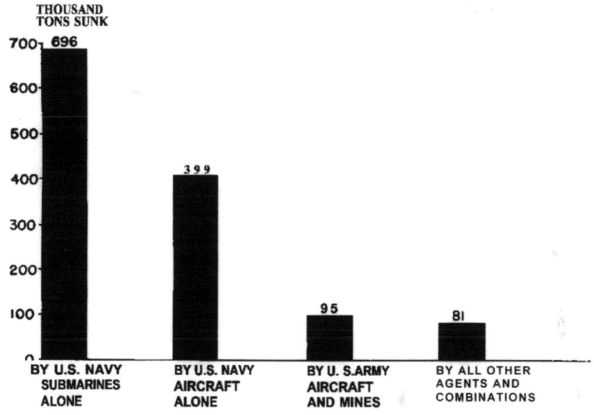

"Japanese Tanker losses:"

Only submarine and naval aircraft were persistently able to reach the (inner zone) shipping lanes, where most of the Japanese were routed.

The chart shows the resultant losses that deprived the Japanese military machine of desperately needed resources and supplies, to continue its' war effort.

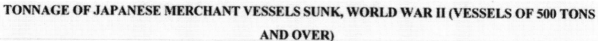

TONNAGE OF JAPANESE MERCHANT VESSELS SUNK, WORLD WAR II (VESSELS OF 500 TONS AND OVER)

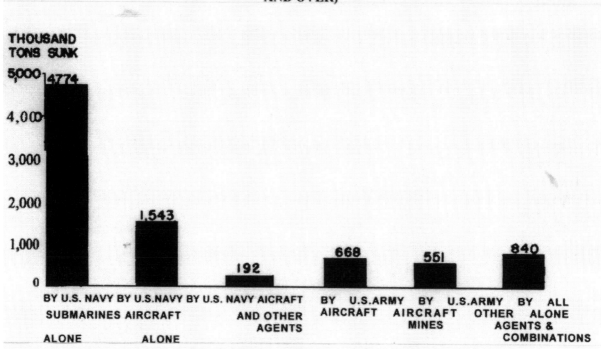

"Japanese Merchant Vessels Sunk"

Submarines alone accounted for 54% of sinkings; naval aircraft alone, 18%. Navy units participated in 77 % of all sinkings and were sole agents in 76% the principal elements represented in the last bar are losses to the British Empire, Netherlands forces and marine casualties.

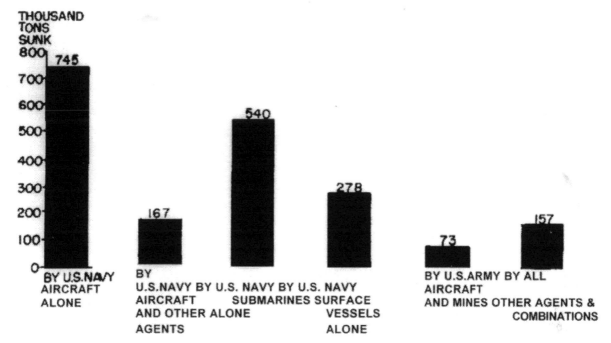

"Warship Tonnage Sunk"

The predominance of United States Naval forces, particularly in the destruction of the Japanese Fleet is clearly illustrated above. United States Naval units alone accounted for 85 % of all sinkings and participated with other forces in an additional 5%. Naval aircraft alone accounted for 38 % and participated in an additional 8%.

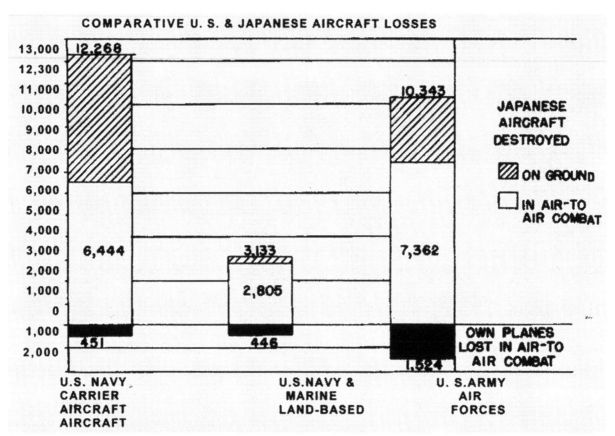

COMPARATIVE U. S. & JAPANESE AIRCRAFT LOSSES

"Comparative Aircraft Losses"

    Japanese losses are based on the best available United States, Army, and Navy figures, although it is impossible to check those figures from Japanese sources. They are believed to be approximately correct.

    Japanese aircraft destroyed by British Empire and Netherlands Air Forces are not included.

"F4U Corsair losses, Gilbert / Marshall's area Combat, non Combat issues"

Date	Model	Mfg#	Squadron	Origin	Destination	Pilot
1/3/44	F4U-1A	18059	VMF-113	Kwajalein Island	Cent. Pacific	
1-25-44		17833	VMF-422	Tarawa Funafuti Island	Cent. Pacific	Lt. R.P. Moran
		17945				Maj. J.S. McLaughlin
		17990				Lt. W.A Aycrigg
		18015				Lt. C.F. Lauesen
		18025				Capt. J.F. Rogers
		10854				Lt. E.C. Thompson
		10875				Lt. T.U. Thurnaw
		18079				Lt. W.A. Wilson
		18116				Capt. C.R. Jeans
		55807				Lt. R.C. Lehnert
		55817				
		55818				
		55825				
		55869	VF-88			
		55872	VMF-422			
		55883				
		55886				
		55892				
		55906				
2/13/44	F4U-2	2617	VMF-532	Makin Island		Lt. Pfizenmaier
2/23/44	F4U-2	2632	VMF-532	Roi Island		Lt. Dolhonde
2/28/44	F4U-1	3826	VMF-422	Apamana Island		1st.Lt.T.W.Thurnaw
3/2//44	F4U-1A	55918	VMF-113	Makin Island		2nd.Lt.C.B.Prather
3/6/44		55823	*********	Engebi Island		1st.Lt.L.R.Johnson
3/9/44		17947	*********	Kwajalien Is.		
		17558				

Date	Type	Number	Squadron	From	To	Pilot
3/26/44		17995	VMF-441	Roi Island	Wotje. Island	Capt.L.E.Midkiff
4/4/44		17926	VMF-311			1st.Lt.R.A.Neuendorf
4/7/44		18056	VMF-422	Enewetak Island	Ponape Island	1st.Lt.W.T.Reardon
		18183				1st.Lt.D.K.Skillikorn
4/13/44		55836	VMF-113	Engebi Island		Maj. W.M. Watkins
4/14/44	F4U-2	2624	VMF-532	Enewetak Island		1st.Lt.J.E.Bonner
		2733			Ponape Island	1st.Lt.D.W.Spatz
	F4U-1A	17817	VMF-441	Roi Island	Cent. Pacific	1st.Lt.J.A.Mitchell
4/23/44		17497	VMF-311	Kwajalein Island		1st.Lt.F.C.Hawkes
5/5/44		49935	VMF-422	Roi Island		2nd.Lt.T.W.Schroeder
5/22/44		17566	VMF-441			1st.Lt.H.Pickering
	F4U-2	2709	VF-101			
5/25/44	F4U-1A	17783	VMF-441		Wotje Island	1st.Lt.R.K.McAllister
5/26/44	F4U-A	56302	VMF-224	Wotje Island		1st.Lt.V.A.Dempsy
		49988	VMF-311		Cent. Pacific	1st.Lt.G.W.Kiemer
5/28/44		55803	VMF-111	Majuro Island	Makin Island	Capt.A.M.Blackman
		18115				2nd.lt.J.E.Thelen
6/2/44	F4U-2	17478	VMF-532	Engebi Island	Cent. Pacific	
6/7/44	F4U-1A	4950	VMF-111	Makin Island	Mille. Island	
6/8/44		17549	VMF-441	Roi Island	Maloelap Is.	2nd.Lt.J.M.Glover
		17790				2nd.Lt.T.Wyatt
6/11/44		55830	VMF-113	Engebi Island	Cent. Pacific	1st.Lt.J.E.Zoellner
6/15/44		56380	VMF-224	Roi Island	Wotje Island	Capt. Tucker
6/16/44		56004		Kwajalein Is.	Cent. Pacific	Lt. Attebery

Date		Number	Squadron	From	To	Pilot
6/20/44		18120	VMF-111	Makin Island	Mille Island	1st.Lt.W.F.Pimlott
6/24/44		50163	VMF-113	Roi Island	Wotje Island	
		49880	VMF-441			1st.LTJ. M. Nolan
6/27/44		55998	VMF-113			Lt. R.H. Zehner
		55866				Capt. G.H. Franck
6/29/44		49734	VMF-441	Roi Island	Cent. Pacific	
		56083	VMF-311			
7/7/44		50056	VMF-422	Engebi Island	Wotje Island	1st.Lt.D.H.Stout
		18055	VMF-111	Mille Island	Cent. Pacific	1st.Lt.Howard T Burris
7/11/44		17786	VMF-441	Roi Island	Wotje Island	
7/12/44		56239	VMF-311			Capt. M.J. Ourran
7/17/44		56001	VMF-113			
7/18/44		49924		Roi Island	Taroa Island	2nd.Lt.G.H.Werts
		55973				1st.Lt.L.W.Johnson
		49997				Maj. R.B. Erskins
7/26/44		17913	VMF-441	Kwajalein Island	Cent. Pacific	1st.Lt.J.W.Robinson
7/30/44		49836	VMF-311	Roi Island	Wotje Island	Capt.M.J.Ourran
8/4/44		17781	VMF-422	Enewetak Island	Cent. Pacific	2nd.Lt.R.V.Schroeder
		49902	VMF-441	Kwajalein Island		2nd.Lt P. Cone. Elmo
8/11/44		18080	VMF-422	Enewetak Island		Lt. E. E. Wolverton
8/18/44		56355	VMF-442			
8/19/44		55814	VMF-442			1ST.Lt.D.A.Dahlquist
8/20/44		56113	VMF-224	Enewetak Island		
8/23/44		56025	VMF-441	Majuro Island	Mille Island	2nd.Lt.K.B.Chambers
8/29/44		50184	VMF-111	Makin Island		1st.LT.J.F.Moore
9/4/44		49446	VMF-441	Roi Island	Cent. Pacific	1st.Lt.Frank L. Moiser
9/8/44		49980	VMF-111	Makin Island		
9/21/44		50202	CASU-30	Majuro Island		

Date	Type	Number	Unit	From	To	Pilot
10/8/44		56095	VMF-224	Enewetak Island	Jaluit Island	Maj.B.S.Clusen
10/9/44		49809	VMF-441	Roi Island	Cent. Pacific	Lt. James M. Vreeland
10/11/44		50392	VMO-155	Majuro Island		Maj. F.S. Hoffecker
10/19/44		56031	VMF-224	Roi Island		Lt.R.E.Longerson
10/21/44		49743	VMF-441			Lt. Robertson Ross
10/24/44		50207	VMF-111	Makin Island	Jaluit Island	2nd.Lt. D. l. Knutson
11/4/44		50511	VMO-115	Kwajalein Island	Western Pac. Area.	
11/5/44		57167	MAG-31	Roi. Island		Capt. Frank Mick
11/5/44		49778	VMF-224			Lt. Francis M. Fox
11/5/44	F4U-1D	50498	VFM-441		Wotje Island	Lt.Richard Stevenson
11/8/44	F4U-1A	49671	VMF-111	Kwajalein Island	Western Pac. Area	
11/9/44		49854	VMF-311	Roi Island		Capt. J.W. Blakeney
11/13/44		56374	VMF-224			
11/18/44	F4U-1D	50508	VMF-113	Engebi Island		
11/27/44		50642	MAG-31	Roi Island		Lt Phillip E. Conroy Jr.
11/29/44		50514	VMBF-231	Majuro Island		Lt. John. D. Harvley Jr.
12/4/44		14508	VMF-224	Roi Island		2nd. Russell Torgerson
12/11/44		50394	VMF-422	Enewetak Island		2nd.Lt. Arthur Wagner
12/19/44		50497	VMF-441	Roi Island		2nd.Lt.John Dalton
		50396				
		50495				
12/22/44	F4U-1A	50027	SVR. -22	Engebi Island		
1/3/45		49741	VFM-111	Roi Island		
		49888		Kwajalein Island		

Date	Type	Number	Squadron	Location		Pilot
1/4/45	F4U-1D	57455	MAG-31			1ST.Lt.E.G. Trembley
1/7/45		57359	VFMB-331	Majuro Island		2nd.Lt.Chester.M.Jerot
1/11/45		50409	SVRN-22	Engebi Island		
/12/45		50371	**VMO-155**	Kwajalein Is.		1ST.Lt.James B. Black
1/16/45		50622	VMF-133	Engebi Island		2nd.Lt.Robert E. Paulin
1/24/45		50377	VMF-113			2nd.Lt.John L. Scott
1/25/45		57348	VMF-422	Engebi Island		
2/11/45		57295	VMF-441	Kwajalein Is.		
2/12/45		50386	VMF-155	Majuro Island		Lt. Harry J. Werner
2/16/45		82181	VMF-311	Roi Island		2nd.Lt. John H. Newton
3/4/45		57300	VMF-422	Engebi Island		2$^{nd.}$Lt.Robert J. Mors
3/8/45		57373	SVR-13	Majuro Island		1st.Lt.Wilbert H. Gieseke
3/15/45	F4U-1A	56100	Mag-13			1st.Lt. E.M. Herrin
3/17/45	F4U-1D	75378	VMF-111	Enewetak Island		2nd.Lt. Fred J. Schwetje
3/26/45		76633	VMF-442			1st.Lt. Kellenberger
4/3/45		57404		Engebi Island		
						42 total lost in action
						High loss Wotje-21
						This area of the pacific!
						********************
						Total loss from all cause accidents combat action: 1,902
5/26/44	F4U-1A	49988	VMF-331	Roi Island		Lt. George Dietmer

"Suggestions and Innovation"

Among the innovations evolving during the early days of the CASU, on ROI was a Spark Plug Bushing Driver by Machinist Guyman, G.R. Winchell AOM1/c AMM1/c converted a fifty caliber-belting machine into a 20- mm belting machine.

AMM1/c Craig Cronin design and worked out a gas cap wrench to facilitate the removal of gas caps from aircraft, Chief D.C. May took parts from a broken Cletrac, mounted them on a flat bed trailer, and then constructed a mobile unit for the Plane Pool,

It carried a compressor, lighting facilities, and a grinding machine. The bombing which CASU underwent February 12, 1944 knocked out a large part of supplies, including the radar test truck and the mobile shop.

Great difficulty was experienced in getting replacements for these vital units, and it was several months before tools, and equipment were procured to enable the CASU to perform its normal mission.

Another problem was experienced everywhere of course, the lack keeping enough rolling stock in operation, a shortage of certain parts such as ignition wire, distributor caps, spark plugs and points.

The shortage necessitated cannibalization of some units and extreme caution in the use of the equipment available.

! To those who made the ultimate sacrifice, while battling the enemy, may Your sleep be peaceful, and eternal!

APPENDICES

CASU PERSONNEL WOUNDED IN BOMBING, FEBRUARY 12 1944 WOUNDED AND EVACUATED

BROWN, Charles Lt. (jg) A-V (S) -USNR -271872
WATSON, Robert L., Ensign A-V (S) - USNR -267780
ROGERS, James C, CHIEF GUNNER, (T) - USN
CARTER Hulbert Earl, 351-07-69, - AM3/C -USN
CATO, Donald Stanley, 623-58-01, -AOM3/C - USNR
COOMBS, Raymond Efferson, 245-12-64 -AMM3/C-USN
DICKMAN, Bruce Leroy, 883-21-85- AMM2/C- USNR
EULITT, Roy Otis, 614-35-80 -PHM1/C- USNR
FITZGERALD, John Patrick, 853-72-27- S2/C -USNR
FOWLER, Dwight Baker, 291-21-86- AOM2/C -USN
HUGILL, John Charles, 883-21-86 S2/C USNR
HULL, Hollis Clare, 655-17-64 -AMM1/C - USNR

KEITH, Albert James, 853-65-60 - S2/C - USNR
KLINT, Warren Theodore, 725-25-32 - AOM2/C- USNR
LARSON, Avery Carr, 409-72-63 - S2/C -USNR
LINTERS, Irving Alexander, 409-72-63 - S2/C -USNR
MEEHAN, Joseph Francis, Jr., 706-85-29- AMM3/C -USNR
O'LEARY, Howard James, 565-15-12- S 2/C -USNR
OVERSTREET, Jack David, 659- 26-81 -AMM3/C- USNR
RADAR, Jessey Leroy, 892-23-95 -S2/C-USNR
RICKS, Owen Luther, 886-33-22- S2/C- USNR
SCHMIDT, Robert Joseph, 223-98-32- AMM2/C -USN
SEARLS, Clarence, Lee, 632-88-16 -AOM2/C- USNR
SELLMAN, Jack Edward, 361-74-80- AMM3/C -USN
SIMS, Joseph, (N) 224-22-05- PR2/C -USN
WHITE, Ralph Leroy, 654-75-92- AOM2/C -USNR
LEBLANC, Lionel John, JR, 645-74-92- AMM2/C- USNR
REGAL, Carl Marion, AMM3/C -575-25-08-USNR

WOUNDED
JACOBY, Ben E., lt. MC (V) G, USNR 172650
COPE, Robert Randall, Ensign, A-V (S), and USNR 231237
ACQUEFRESCA, Louis Edward, 212-79-69-AMM1/C
SASTON, William Joseph, 413-55-52-AMM2/C-USN
BALL, George Kruse, 845-31-31- SK3/C-USNR
BONOGARO, Salvatore, 608-66-29-AMM3/C-USNR
BROWN, Jasper Samuel, 262-45-48-AMM1/C-USN
DOYLE, Marvin James, 648-08-76-AMM3/C-USNR
DUDLEY, Walter Sexton, 629-17-59-AMM3/C-USNR
FEIUMAN, Leslie Raymond, 653-65-86-S2/C-USNR
FERRIS, Stephen Joseph, 203-96-98-ARM2/C-USNR
GEBHARDT, Gilbert, (N) 853-55-99-S2/C-USNR
GOODING, Vincent George 665-66-64-PHM3/C-USN
HENDERSON, David Carlton, 410-50-29-AMM1/C-USN
HEPTINC, Alvin Howard, 645-65-81-AMM3/C-USNR
HOLERIN, Bernard, (N) 870-36-46-S2/C-USNR
HOCK, Edward Walter, 853-69-24-USNR
HOYLES, John William, 311-24-35-ACMM (AA) - USN
JARRELL, Christopher Hoyt, 378-44-27-S2/C- USN
KELSEY, Merrill Hartt, 402-97-35-AMM1/C-USNR
KNACKSTEDT, Virgil Yvonne, 553-03-87-ART2/C-USNR
KRENEK, Joseph Russell 853-67-63-S2/C-USNR

LEONARD,   Myren   Davis,   866-45-07-S2/C-USNR
Listed as wounded in the attached
LIVELY, Gilbert Alvin, 853-57-49-S2/C-USNR

The Purple Heart was awarded to all those wounded during
The attack, and bombing.

LOGAN, John Jackson, 409-29-09-AMM1/C-USNR
LOPEMAN, Cecil Edward, 618-58-52-PTR2/C-USNR
MANNING, Eddie (N) 377-41-68-PTRPTR2/C-USNR
NELSON, Norman Alexander, 306-62-98-AMM2/C-USNR
POLLOCK, John Howard, 723-22-17-AMM3/C-USNR
PUGH, Tasse, (N) 671-55-45- AMM3/C-USNR
RANDOLPH, George Franklin, Jr., 401-47-46-USNR
REEDY, Paul Francis, 853-36011-S2/C-S2/C-USNR
SCHOFELD, THOMAS Jefferson, 191-03-86-ACOM (AA) USNR
WEATZ, Ervin Alfred, 611-03-46-PTR3/C-USNR

AWARDS AND CITATIONS TO PERSONAL OF CASU (20)

BROWN, Jasper S., ACMM, USN --------------- Presidential Unit Citation
BELLES, Richard J., ACOM USN---------------Presidential Unit Citation
*EDGE, Noial P., CY, USN****************Presidential Unit Citation*
*STEPNOWSKI, Leon Adam, ACRM, USN***Air Medal*
*JACOBY, Ben "E", Lt. MC, USNR *********Silver Star*
To the officers and men of CASU (F) 20 of the First and Second
*Echelons*****Asiatic-Pacific Ribbon**** *with one Star*
****

A comment on my research and contact with people, that I have had the pleasure of sharing information with, during my years of research into this project.

I have had the pleasure of reading many articles, and or books regarding war experiences from many sources. Pilots, Crewmembers, Officers and enlisted personnel. I must say, that a trend began to show itself, especially among Pilots in their descriptions of their combat accounts, always seem to exclude their ground support people, in the documents.

I realize that those combat exploits they were involved in were theirs alone, (Fighter Pilots) but without the dedication of the ground crews, along with the many tiring hours involved in their efforts, many into the early morning hours of the night, to ensure that those aircraft were in the best condition for their effort into the next days combat flights. Theirs, after all, were to be part of the team to make the dangerous air sorties a success, and to shorten the war!

During my years of service, my contact, with commissioned officers, was at best minimal, for as stated, within the pages of this book, mostly in the nighttime hours were spent alone. While working the daylight hours, your work details were given by persons with ratings, that were superior to yours, so anyone outside the group, that was commissioned, would have been contacted by the Chief Petty officer in charge of division.

I only had one incident, during my navy years, which involved contact with a Commissioned Officer, which left me with a bad memory.

On arriving back in the United States, after the bombing of my ship, while waiting for transfer to Mare Island ship yard, where repairs on the ship were to be made, a good portion of the crew was temporally station at Treasure Island Receiving Station.

A fellow crewmember, Robert H'idalgo and myself went on liberty in San Francisco, California. We were walking down the street, window-shopping, we came to a Jewelry Store and became interested in some of the items displayed in the windows. As we preceded more toward the doorway and entrance to the store, we were approached by a couple of Shore Patrol members (Military Police.) They told us that an Officer had complained to them that we had deliberately ducked inside this storefront to avoid saluting him, which left us stunned. We explained to the two, Shore Patrol members, that we hadn't even been aware of his presence in the area. They informed us that the Officer had filed a complaint with them and they had no choice, but to place us under arrest and return us to our base. As a result of this incident, we were placed on restriction and denied liberty for the next two weekends.

Acknowledgement

During those difficult war years, from 1941until the end of hostilities in 1945, there were literally tens of thousands, Military Personal, positioned at every sector that was involved in this great struggle upon this planet earth.
Many different units, that were formed from the various military groups, whether, Army, Navy, Marines, or Air force, were at different locations around this globe.

Here, in the South and Central Pacific, were hundreds of Navy Military Units, stationed in this great expanse of ocean, which covered thousands of endless miles of open space.

This unit, CASU (F) 20 was a part of this great struggle to help free this world, from the grasp, of these nations that would impose their will and dominance over us, and in the end to enslave the free people of the world.

I wish to give thanks to the many friends, sailors and others, that have come forward with there reminisces and memories, from their war years, as a part of CASU (f) 20 during, and after the ordeal of February, 12 1944.

I do respect their involvement in this project. Unlike many people that were part of that struggle and performed their tasks, I wish to leave a lasting verifiable record, from their own accounts and personal memories, that happened those many years ago, and also of mine.

I have spent the last 6 to 8 years, doing my research, on this book. Much of this documentation comes, as a result of research into the National Archive documents.

All statements and personal accounts of events, actions, and happenings that were given to me, I believe to be true and accurate, as to each person's memories. Some may disagree, with other versions or stories; I have no control over that.

Many units were there, on Roi-Namur, during those years, but only on one or two occasions, did I stray from the CASU, history. Once again, I wish to give my deepest thanks to all of the people that contributed to this project.

Bill Armstrong!

I wish to express, my love and thanks to my wife, Ann for her support, and help over the many months leading up to the completion of this document.

I am sure that without the prompting, and encouragement offered during these long, and sometimes trying times, have made this task far easier than it would have been without her!

Made in the USA
Charleston, SC
16 February 2012